KNOWING HE'S THERE

True Stories of God's Subtle Yet Unmistakable Touch

CHARLES SACCHETTI

Acknowledgment

My sincere gratitude to Samantha Simoneau for performing over and above the call of duty as she painstakingly edited the manuscript. Working with her was both a pleasure and a valuable learning experience. It's a blessing that our paths crossed.

Dedication

To the readers of this book, whether they have recognized God's touch or not. If they have, may they continue to rejoice. If they haven't, may they soon receive that blessing.

Foreword

The following stories are true. My wish is that they serve two purposes: The first is that you thoroughly enjoy them, and when you are finished, you will feel happier and more light-hearted than when you began. The second is that they serve as a catalyst to help you recognize God's loving touch in your day-to-day walk.

At the age of 22, I had been at Basic Training for a few weeks. It was about midnight on May 16th, 1970, during a night-training session at the U.S. Army base, Fort Leonard Wood, Missouri. We were out in the woods, about five miles from our barracks. It was a clear, moonlit night. Since it was now Sunday morning, our chaplain announced that he would conduct a Sunday service, and all were invited to attend. About 20 soldiers gathered together and followed the chaplain to a small clearing.

The chaplain set up his "altar" on the hood of a Jeep. The service lasted about a half-hour. During the service, I remember looking up at the sky and seeing thousands of stars, along with the brilliantly shining moon. Out there, among the trees and sounds of the deep woods, in the middle of the night and humbly attired in muddy fatigues, I experienced the most spiritual service I had ever attended. I truly felt the presence of God.

I will never forget it.

Table of Contents

1

Spinner

Spinner's 1963 Corvair Monza

I HAVE SOMETIMES thought of Our Lord as the great conductor of His world, being the initial cause that orchestrates wonderful and glorious events. As I consider my life, I can clearly see evidence of this. Over 60 years ago, something happened that was a necessary precursor which allowed me to progress to this stage of my life. And I sincerely believe that God's hand put that event into motion.

That's where "Spinner" enters the picture.

I never had a big brother until 1955, when I met the Safety Patrol kid at his post on the corner of 63rd Street and Buist Avenue in southwest Philadelphia. At the age of 11, Tommy Manieri was a gangly kid, almost six feet tall, which meant he towered over me, a skinny eight-year-old. We'd chat every day, and he soon invited me to join his baseball team, the Southwest Colts. That was the start of a friendship that has endured to this day, over six decades later.

We had a lot of fun in those days. We would go to the matinee movies at the Benn Theater on Saturday afternoons. If you were under 13, the ticket cost you a quarter. If not, it was 35 cents. Tommy had to bring his birth certificate with him. Since he was so tall, the lady at the ticket window never believed he was only 11. Back in those days, the extra 10 cents bought a Tastykake Pie, so he didn't mind going through the trouble of proving his age. There was also the time when we missed our ride to our baseball game. Tommy had a bike. I didn't. So, without hesitation, he told me to get onto the handlebars, and he peddled the two miles to the ball field at 58th Street and Whitby Avenue. Although he was a bit tired, he still got three hits in the game and made a great catch in center field. The ride home was a happy one.

During the summer months, after engaging in some highly competitive games of stickball or half-ball, we would invariably climb the gray, wooden steps that led to the shaded landing at the rear of Tommy's house. After drinking a tall glass of ice water dispensed from his mom's large, glass pitcher, four of us would engage in a few games of Pinochle. This was strictly for bragging rights. In fact, I am still proud to say that, one afternoon, while playing against Tommy and our buddy, Franny Kehoe, my partner, Gary Teears, and I pulled a record 73-point hand, an amazing feat. I feel very confident that this record still stands after six decades, especially since no one has played cards up there for over 50 years. Another thing happened, in 1960, that has left a permanent mark on our friendship. One year earlier, the animated series *Clutch Cargo* began running in Philadelphia. Clutch, the protagonist, was the mentor to a young friend named "Spinner." I thought that Tommy looked like Spinner, so I started calling him that. To this day, when I call him on the phone, it's not "Hiya, Tom," it's, "Whaddya say, Spinner?"

But Spinner was a special kid for another reason. His mom, Floy, his dad, Rocco, and his brother, Jerry, were all deaf. Spinner was hearing impaired but could hear with the help of hearing aids. Besides the ability to sign to communicate with his family, he was a wonderful lip-reader. Aside from the obvious practical benefits of this talent, it came in quite handy when we would watch a Phillies game on TV. On more than one occasion, Spinner would tell us what was being said during some great "rhubarbs" between Manager Gene Mauch and various umpires. This was really "inside baseball" stuff.

As you can see, Spinner overcame a lot of adversity as a kid and, along with his family, was a person we all admired. He did not consider his physical impairment a handicap, it was just something to overcome and deal with. As our childhood years flew by, he met a sweet young lady from the neighbor-hood and became the first one of us to get married. He tied the knot with Margie Ronan in October of 1966 at the age of 21. After only a few years of married life, he would face his toughest challenge yet. In the spring of 1970, his beloved mother and brother were killed in an automobile accident on the Schuylkill Expressway. Jerry died on Valentine's Day, and Floy lasted until March 14th before she succumbed to her injuries. Her funeral is forever embedded in my mind, as I left that same day to travel to Clearwater, Florida, to begin my professional baseball career. That was a bittersweet flight. Throughout this ordeal, Spinner and Rocco were pillars of strength and dignity.

Aside from my faith, the best things in my life, my family, my sales career, and many dear friends, are connected, either directly or indirectly, to my baseball career. Spinner was the person God sent to get that started. Always looking out for me, in 1964, he suggested that I borrow his beloved 1963 Corvair Monza for my driver's test. He figured it would be much more maneuverable than my father's big 1957 Dodge Coronet with no power steering. He was right, of course, and I passed the test on the first shot! Nowadays, he lets me "borrow" his mind on a regular basis. You see, Spinner is also D. Thomas Manieri, tax accountant extraordinaire, based in Cape May Court House, New Jersey. We meet regularly for business and pleasure. After all of these years, Spinner is still taking care of the little kid he met on the corner of 63rd and Buist Avenue. The only difference is, back then, he made it safe for me to cross the street. Now he makes it safe for me to file my tax return!

2

Uncle Mario

Pvt. Mario Sacchetti at age 18

I SUPPOSE, AS you get older, you tend to look back on your life and appreciate all of the blessings that God has provided. At least that is the case with me. And, as I do so, it becomes very clear to me how much my immediate and extended family has impacted me and given me moments to cherish. Regarding my extended family, I'd have to say that my father's brother, my Uncle Mario Sacchetti, has provided the most of these memorable moments.

Mario was the youngest of the four Sacchetti brothers and was born in 1925 to Grand Pop Crescenzo and Grand Mom Maria Sacchetti. He preceded one girl, Pia, who was born two years later. Mario was five inches taller than any of his siblings, standing almost 6' 2" when fully grown. As a kid, he was very thin, and his buddies said he resembled the hands of a clock, so they called him "six o'clock." He was a good athlete, playing baseball for BOK Technical High School in south Philadelphia, and was the only one of the siblings to graduate.

All of this being said, it is the man Uncle Mario became after this time who had the biggest effect on me.

He was drafted into the Army during WWII, at the age of 18. As a 19-year-old tail gunner on the B-17 Flying Fortress, he participated in the invasion of Normandy on D-Day, June 6th, 1944. On April 29th, 1945, he assisted in the liberation of the dreaded Dachau concentration camp. Uncle Mario rarely, if ever, spoke of his military service. As we grew closer, during my teenage years, I came to realize how those memories had affected him. He came away from those experiences a more introspective, sensitive person. Once, when I asked him what he remembered most about the war, he described how wonderful it was one night, in an English meadow, when he was able to read the newspaper by only the light of the full moon. This was not the answer I expected, but I understood his need to find something good in what was surely a living hell for a nice, friendly teenager from 9th and Moore Streets. He never missed church on Sunday, ever thankful for having come home safely.

To say Uncle Mario had his quirks would be an understatement. A bachelor until the age of 42, he was a frequent, welcome dinner guest at all of his married siblings' homes. One of his trademark moves was to sit next to one of us kids and hijack a meatball off of our plates if we had the bad judgment to turn our heads and join in a conversation. An admission of guilt was never forthcoming. Uncle Mario used to enjoy riding with me on my Vespa. It was quite a sight, that big guy on the rear seat as we typically drove to shop for bargains at the nearest E. J. Korvette or Klein's department store. We would frequently go out for breakfast on Saturday mornings. That was an experience in itself. He had his favorite spots, and the waitresses all wanted to take care of him because he was a very generous tipper. We would walk in, and the waitress would have his large, take-out-size cup of coffee on the table before we even sat down. The regular cups were too small, hence the larger take-out cup. He **NEVER** let me pay the tab, even when I was a college graduate and working. I was still his nephew, and that's the way it was. On the occasions when we would try a new restaurant, I'd ask him where he would prefer to sit, and he would say, "Anywhere is ok." I'd pick a spot, and he'd always tell me it was no good!

Quirky!

Uncle Mario was an avid card player, coin collector, and opera lover. No one else in the family liked opera, even a little, and we all told him how strange he was for enjoying it. That didn't faze him one bit, and every Sunday afternoon, he'd listen to Puccini, Verdi, or one of his other favorites. He generously tipped the bank tellers he knew, so he had no trouble getting bags of pennies, quarters, or half dollars to sift through in search of rare coins. He would play poker a few nights a week, with his buddies, until the wee hours of the morning. He usually won a few bucks, but he greatly enjoyed playing with his brothers and father for only bragging rights. His beloved wife, Rita, passed away in March of 1982, and he remained widowed for 29 years. To combat the loneliness, Mario would take daily bus rides to Atlantic City, where he held his own at the poker tables.

As one of the few people on earth who actually liked my joke-telling, it was not unusual for me to call him during the evening, while away on business, to share a good joke I had heard. He had a unique delayed reaction after I delivered the punchline. One or two seconds would elapse, and then he would break out into a hearty laugh that might last for a whole minute. Admittedly, I had a reputation to live up to, so I wouldn't tell him a joke unless I thought it met my "high standards" (groan). On more than one occasion, while riding in the car, he would abruptly start laughing after recalling a joke I had told him weeks earlier. Now, *that's* an audience!

As Mario and I grew older, I came to appreciate and love him as more of a second father than an uncle. He passed away at

86, and I had the privilege of being his advocate and the over-seer of his medical care in his later years. I considered this role both an honor and a blessing. He provided a lot of great times for all of us, and I just loved spending time with him.

I have even learned to appreciate opera … now and then.

3

Pinch Me, I'm Dreaming

Craigsville, Virginia

IN THE SUMMER of 1966, as a freshman at Temple University, I had an adventure. My baseball coach, Skip Wilson, gave a teammate and me the opportunity to play summer ball for the Craigsville Cardinals, a team in the Valley League, which took its name from the beautiful Shenandoah Valley of Virginia where it was based. The league consisted of seven teams, each one representing a local town. The players, all of high quality, were mostly southern, playing for teams from places like Clemson, North Carolina, and Southern Illinois. This would be a real challenge for me, as it would give me the chance to compete against some of the best college players in the country. I was set to make the trip with one of my team-mates and was told the bus ride would last about seven hours. We would be provided with day jobs and play our games every night, sometimes traveling 90 miles one way. I was also told that the academic year at Temple ended about two weeks later than most of the southern schools, so the league would have already started by the time we arrived. What this meant was that Craigsville would already have a starting team, so I would have to play my way into the lineup by showing the coach that I could perform better than his current second baseman. I was up for the challenge, so I said, "Let's get the show on the road!"

Our Greyhound bus left Philly about 2:00 p.m. The projected seven-hour trip ultimately took 10 hours. The bus doubled as a postal truck, and it seemed like it stopped every half-hour to pick up bags of mail. After finally arriving, we were greeted by the coach, whose first words to us were: "Who's who? Who's who?" This guy was, shall we say, a bit "eccentric." Although it was midnight, he was still dressed in his baseball uniform and reminded me of Sergeant Carter from *Gomer Pyle, U.S.M.C.* After tossing us our uniforms, he said, "Ok, boys, now I'm gonna take you to your place to stay." I was very tired and couldn't wait to get to bed. I didn't expect the Marriott Residence Inn, but I wasn't quite prepared for what I was about to see. We stopped at a gas station and then exited the car. Behind the station, I noticed a little one-room building about the size of a two-car garage. "Well, here you go," the coach announced. We unlocked the door and saw two cots, no running water or bathroom, and only a small table and chair to enhance the ambiance. We would have to use the shower and bathroom in the gas station, whose proprietor also owned our shack. We were on our own for meals. The coach left, and my teammate said, "You gotta be kidding. I'm going home." A day or so later, he did.

My job was working as a laborer at the construction site of a new Boy Scout Camp in nearby Goshen. I was paid $40 per week. I awoke at 5:00 a.m., started work by 6:00, and quit at 2:30. Then I went back to the shack and rested before going to the ballpark. I did not play in my first four games. As I said earlier, the season had begun, and the coach had his lineup set. About a week in, he had me pinch-hit, and I hit a double in the 8th inning. I started the next game, had two hits, and then I was in the lineup as a regular and hitting the ball very well.

After being there two weeks, I was preparing for batting practice before the game when a nice, elderly lady came up to the fence and said, "Are you the boy from Temple?"

"Yes, ma'am," I replied.

"Well, my sister had put up the boys from Temple a few years ago, and they were very nice. Her husband died last year, so she didn't do it, but now she said, if you're interested, you could stay with her."

I thought I had just met an angel. **Anything** was better than my shack, so I quickly said, "Yes, ma'am. Thank you." She arranged to pick me up that night and take me to her sister's place.

I thought I had died and gone to heaven! I was taken to a beautiful mansion, on the side of the mountain, and shown to my own knotty-pine bedroom with a view of their cattle grazing on the hillside. It turned out these folks were one of the wealthiest families in Virginia and probably the nicest. Among other things, they owned a Ford dealership and had a staff of folks who took care of the cattle. Margaret, my host, was a wonderful, elderly lady who insisted that I join her for the great, home-cooked meals she prepared. I pinched myself more than once for the first couple of weeks and found out it wasn't a dream after all. Margaret was a gift from God, who delivered me from a very uncomfortable situation.

The season was going well, and I was on a hot hitting streak when I came down with a terrible case of poison oak from working in the woods. Since I was playing so well, I figured I had a little leverage to try an idea I had. I went to the team's sponsor, a local insurance broker, and said, "Sir, I love playing for this team, but look at this poison oak I caught. The doctor said I have to stay out of the woods because I am very susceptible. If I don't work, I'll have to go home."

He replied, "You don't want to do that, boy. Let me see what I can do."

I found out that hitting .340 had its perks. My job changed from being a laborer in the hot sun for eight hours a day at $40 per week to the newly formed position of Caretaker of the ball field. I would work from 10:00 a.m. to 2:00 p.m. for $50 per week. My duties included picking up the trash and lining the baselines for the games. Most of the local kids played on the field during the day, so I hit them pop-ups and pitched to them at batting practice in exchange for their picking up the trash. The base-lining I did myself.

I had a great time that summer. My first experience away, on my own, started out shaky but ended with me making some wonderful new friends and enjoying a great adventure. Over the years, I have often wondered what would have happened if I were only hitting .240 instead of .340 when I caught my case of poison oak!

4

The Half-Dollar Adventure

1965 Vespa Scooter

IN THE SUMMER of 1965, as a recent high school grad, I decided to make a significant purchase. My buddy, Richie Downs, had an old Vespa motor scooter. It gave him a degree of freedom while providing lots of fun. To me, that was a combination that seemed hard to beat, so I plopped down $450 and bought myself a brand-new, red, 125cc, 1965 Vespa. It was manufactured in Italy, by the Piaggio Corporation, so my

Vespa and I appeared to be a marriage made in heaven (or at least Pontedera, Italy). In no time at all, I was scooting all over the place. I'd take it to the store. I'd drive to my baseball games, in full uniform, with glove and spikes set securely in the storage basket under the handlebars. Richie and I even drove our scooters to Wildwood, New Jersey, a shore town about 80 miles from our homes in southwest Philly. At a cruising speed of about 35 mph, and after a stop or two on the way, the trip took about three hours but, heck, we were kids and had all the time in the world. The thing I remember most from that trip is, while riding on the Walt Whitman Bridge, we were almost blown over by passing tractor-trailers, whose drivers had the gall to actually want to drive at the legal speed limit!

When fall came around, it was time to start my classes at Temple University. My buddy, Ronny Wagner, and I made the daily trip on the scooter through some of the toughest neighborhoods in Philadelphia. With Ronny in the seat behind me, we sometimes had to dodge flying objects, wild dogs, and irate cab drivers who, for some reason, resented my buzzer-like horn in their ears when we snuck up on them as they idled in a traffic jam. There was no such thing as a traffic backup for us. I could simply maneuver the scooter between the rows of stacked cars to reach the front of the line. If that didn't work, I would drive up on the sidewalk to avoid the long wait. This technique was illegal, of course, but Ronny was a top-flight lookout, scanning for any cop cars that may have been lurking nearby. Upon arriving at campus, we would park the scooter alongside scores of Honda motorbikes and other Vespas on the Broad Street sidewalk. In the '60s, such vehicles were very popular. It didn't hurt that my gas expenditures averaged about 50 cents every other week and liability insurance only cost $35 per year.

As winter approached, we had to make sure we dressed appropriately for the ride. I would wear a heavy peacoat under a scarf and windbreaker. I had a pair of motorcycle gloves like the Highway Patrol cops had and a woolen stocking cap with goggles. I couldn't afford a windshield. Ronny dressed similarly. Upon arriving at school, we would bolt to the Mitten Hall men's room and get the blood circulating to our faces and hands again with the help of the hot-air hand dryers.

Of course, if there was snow in the forecast, we would resort to more mundane modes of transportation, like bumming a ride in a buddy's car or taking the Broad Street subway. However, sometimes I would be surprised by unexpected weather changes. For example, during freshman-year midterms, I decided to go to my friend's house so we could help each other prepare for our Economics 101 exam. As it was one of the most boring classes ever conceived, with a teacher that matched the excitement level, we reasoned that, between the two of us, we could figure things out. So I rode the scooter to his house, roughly 20 miles away in Havertown, Pennsylvania, and we did our best to be serious students for about an hour. Then break time arrived, so we decided to take a walk to the local basketball courts and play a little one-on-one. The time kind of slipped away, so to speak, and, after two hours of b-ball, we realized it was time to resume our studies, just as the first snowflake began to fall. Naturally, I thought it was wise to get home ASAP, given the ominous-looking sky. On the way home, the snow started to come down harder. As I carefully drove at a snail's pace, I arrived at the top of the hill near the old Gimbels department store at 69ᵗʰ Street. When I began to brake for a red light, the rear of the scooter fishtailed, and down I went, thrown to the ground, landing on my rear end. The scooter went flying but, thanks be to God, both the scooter and I were unharmed.

I continued to drive that Vespa throughout my college career, taking it to daily baseball practice in the spring and then home each evening. Only after having another fall, this time on Girard Avenue near the Philadelphia Zoo, late in my senior year, did I think it might be a good idea to upgrade to other modes of transportation. You see, after slipping and falling on the wet cobblestones and having a tractor-trailer barely miss me, I figured I would give my guardian angel a break, so I sold the scooter.

During my 40-plus years of married life, I have occasionally suggested that I might want to buy another scooter, just for fun and for old times' sake. However, that whim abruptly ends when I do a quick calculation in my head. Besides the cost of a new scooter, now several thousand dollars, there would, no doubt, be the added cost of a decent divorce lawyer.

5

A Strange Noise
at 40,000 Feet

McDonnell Douglas DC-10

I REMEMBER THE first time I stood next to a jetliner. It was in March of 1970, and I was a hopeful baseball player trying to win a job in the Phillies organization. I was on my way from Philadelphia to spring training at Clearwater, Florida. As I approached the plane, I took one look and was amazed that such a big thing could stay up in the air. It did, thank God, and I'm happy to say that, throughout the years, every other one I've been on has done the same. Of course, I attribute this fact to the skills of the pilots, in addition to the rosary I say before each flight! To me, it's very interesting to see how people react to being passengers on a vehicle that's defying gravity thousands of feet in the air. It seems we all have stories to tell of our flying experiences.

When I worked as Temple University's Business Manager of Athletics, it was my job to arrange for every aspect of the various teams' travel. Of all of the sports, football was the greatest challenge because of the number of passengers involved. Among other things, my duties included arranging hotel accommodations, meals, transportation to and from airports, police escorts, transportation for all of the equipment, and, of course, booking the flights themselves. The traveling party typically would number between 75 and 90 players, coaches, administrators, and alumni. It was during this time of my life that I experienced some rather interesting trips into the wild, blue yonder.

In October of 1972, we traveled to Logan Airport in Boston in order to take on Boston University. I chartered a United Airlines Caravelle jet that had a seating capacity of about 90. That evening, after the game, we boarded the plane in a rainstorm for the flight home that was expected to last about an hour. As we took off, the storm got worse, and lightning flashed all around. The small jet was being tossed and shaken, and everybody on the plane was very quiet. I was sitting next to our travel representative from United, and he looked worse than I felt. The plane continued to bounce all around and, when I saw the flight attendants sit down and strap themselves in, I couldn't help but notice the concern on their faces. By then, some of the players were getting sick, and you could hear various prayers filling the cabin. When we arrived in the Philly area roughly two hours later, we circled around for about 30 minutes, waiting for clearance to land. Our little jet was still being tossed around right up until the time our wonderful pilot landed the plane on the runway. After more than a few "Thank you, Lords," we all broke out into immediate applause, and many of the pale faces regained their blood supply. Our 280-pound lineman hugged the pilot as he exited the cockpit. My agent, who had flown almost a million miles in his career, told me it was one of his top five scary flights. My girlfriend at the time was there to pick me up, as we were set to attend a party. I'm not a drinker, but I had a couple that night in an effort to calm down.

In October of 1971, we traveled to Morgantown to play the University of West Virginia. My agent told me we would take a Boeing 727 into Morgantown and depart on a Boeing 737. As we arrived at our destination in a mountainous area, the plane circled around as it prepared for landing. Looking out of the window, I admired the beautiful mountain foliage that surrounded us as we descended. It seemed as if we were in the bottom of a bowl, not able to see the sky above. It was very strange. Suddenly, I felt a bump. I was amazed to find out that we had landed. I then learned that the airport was actually hewn from the top of a lower mountain peak, and the foliage I was observing was that of the higher, surrounding mountains. Before the trip home, I asked the agent why we were taking a different plane, the 737, for the return flight. He calmly said, "We need some extra power to make sure we get over the mountains when we take off."

Ok, that made me feel better!

These episodes aside, one that I'll never forget occurred over the Thanksgiving holiday in 1972. My travel agent gave me the opportunity to accompany him and a group on a five-day junket to London, England, from Wednesday through Sunday. What made this irresistible was the fact that, to thank me for my business, he would allow me and a friend to take the trip at their cost. So I'd be able to take my first international trip for a total of $171, period! This included hotel accommodations, meals, flights, tips, the whole shebang.

The eight-hour, night flight to Heathrow Airport, aboard the DC-10, was a bit tedious, but we were able to kill three hours of it by playing chess. After a nice visit, seeing all of the typical touristy sites, like Piccadilly Circus, the Tower of London, Big Ben, and the Changing of the Guard, we headed to the airport for the trip home. As was the case on the incoming flight, the plane was scheduled to briefly stop at New York on the way. About two hours into the flight, while watching a movie and listening through my earphones, I heard a distinct thumping noise. I had flown many times and yet had never heard such a sound. When we arrived in New York, we were told we would have a two-hour layover so they could "clean" the plane. This seemed strange to me since we only had a short flight to Philly. Who cares if the plane gets cleaned at 2:00 a.m.? Plus, how long does it take to clean a plane? Two hours? As we boarded the plane, I observed that it was spotless. There were no cups, magazines, or other things thrown around, and as I sat down I noticed that all of the earphones were gone.

When I returned to work, I called the agent to thank him for his graciousness and mentioned that we had a wonderful trip. Then I asked him about the strange decision to clean the plane at that time. I heard a stifled laugh. "What's up?" I asked. He then told me that, about two hours into the flight, the plane had lost one of its three engines over the ocean. The plane we took home from New York was a DC-10, all right, but was actually a different plane. Hence, no earphones and, yes, very clean.

Thump, indeed!

I thanked the agent again, this time for not telling me what happened during the flight. I hung up and looked forward to the Thanksgiving turkey with sharp provolone sandwich Mom had made me for lunch.

Up, up, and away!

6

A Loving Heart at Christmas Time

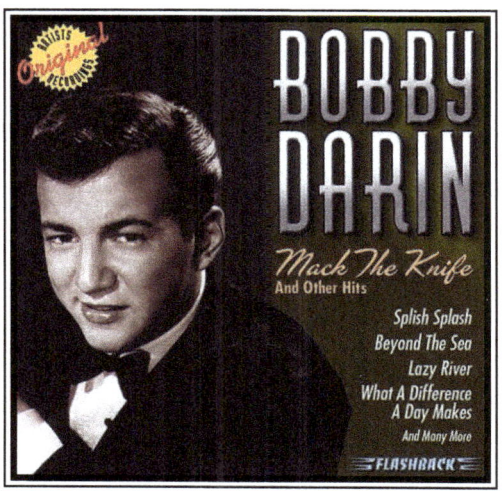

IT ALL STARTED in the spring of 1972. The perks of my job in Temple University's Athletic Department included my use of the facilities on a regular basis. One particular lunch hour, I decided to go out to the tennis courts and practice hitting backhands against the big, green wall outside of McGonigle Hall. After about a half-hour, I felt what is best described as a dull ache in my lower back. Over the next few months, the pain worsened, and I decided to go to the Temple Hospital

Orthopedic Department to find out what, if anything, was wrong. Testing determined that I had a herniated or perhaps a ruptured disk: L5, to be exact. Over the next year or so, my condition worsened, and I underwent the usual treatment. At first, that included exercises, heat therapy, and wearing a back brace during my waking hours.

None of this helped, which led to more aggressive treatments. I had two weeks of bed rest at home, lying on my mattress, which sat on top of a ¾-inch plywood bed board. I was allowed to get out of bed only to shower and use the bathroom. The bed rest didn't help. I was admitted twice to the hospital for several days of "traction," where weights would hang from my feet to relieve pressure on the spine. That didn't help either. Finally, by August of the next year, I would try one last-ditch effort to improve my condition and avoid surgery: I wore a body cast that started at my shoulders and wrapped around my entire torso. The cast was the old-fashioned, plaster-of-Paris kind, hot and heavy, especially in August. I was in that cast for a month, and then we waited three more to see if there was any improvement. There wasn't.

Running out of patience, I spoke with my doctor and said, "I've had enough of this stuff. Let's get the surgery done." Of course, there were no guarantees of success. Back in those days, there weren't any noninvasive, laser surgeries. I would have to be cut to have the disk removed. The disk in question was pressing on the sciatic nerve, which caused my entire left leg to be completely numb, and the pain was a like a toothache that wouldn't go away. The hope was that the surgery would allow the nerve to regenerate over time, and healing would take place.

Doctor and patient were now on the same page, and I checked into room 939 at Temple Hospital on December 19th, 1973. My surgery was set for the 21st. I had an elderly roommate, a Jewish man named David. Dave was there for a heart valve replacement. Although very common now, this procedure was considered to be quite risky back then. Dave was a wonderful old guy, and we talked for hours about our families and agreed to pray for each other's successful outcomes. On the 20th, the day before my surgery, with Dave still snoozing, I quietly turned on my transistor radio to hear the news, and what I heard was shocking: Bobby Darin had just passed away. He had undergone the same surgery Dave was scheduled for and had died from complications. I quickly turned off the radio, thinking that this news was the last thing ol' Dave needed to hear. Fortunately, Dave was still asleep. Every time a nurse came in, I would tell them not to mention anything about Darin's passing, and it was good that Dave didn't like TV. I was able to keep him in the dark.

My parents came to visit that evening. Mom gave me her little statue of the Virgin Mary to keep in the room. That night, Dave asked me about the statue, and I explained that we believe Mary can intercede on our behalf to her Son, Jesus Christ. Since we believe He is the Son of God, it is a no-brainer to ask His mom to help us. Dave had learned that his surgery would also take place the next day. He asked me if I would let him see the statue. I picked it up, gave it a kiss of reverence, and handed it to him. Dave looked at it, smiled, and also gave it a little kiss. He then looked at me and said, "I ain't taking any chances."

Thank God, both of our surgeries were successful. I was

allowed to go home on Christmas Eve. Dave had to stay a few days more. When I hugged him goodbye, it felt like I was leaving a good buddy, even though he was old enough to be my grandfather. As I was leaving, he told me he knew about Bobby Darin, after all. The lady who brought in dinner mentioned it to him while I was napping. He knew I was trying to keep it from him, so he didn't want to make me feel bad by letting on that he knew.

Talk about a man with a good heart!

7

Making the Right Move

IN 1973, AT the age of 25, I received an offer I couldn't refuse. Thankfully, it wasn't from an aging Mafia chieftain! No, this offer was made by a 40-something Irishman, Bud Wilson, the brother of my nationally known and highly respected Temple University baseball coach, Skip Wilson. Bud had an upper-management position at the university's Facilities Department. It just so happened that he would be hiring an assistant, and he approached me with the idea of transferring from my job as Business Manager of Athletics to fill the new position.

The idea interested me for several reasons: First, it would enable me to directly supervise a multi-faceted service department which included the University Post Office, the Driver-Helper unit, the facilities storeroom, and the warehousing operation. This meant that I would be able to utilize some of the management tools I learned at Temple's business school. All of the employees were union workers, so I would be directly involved with union contracts, work rules, and grievance procedures. Secondly, Bud was a guy I knew was street smart and fun to be around. He and Skip had inherited that same gene that allowed them to enjoy life even when the going got tough. And thirdly, the salary was about $3,000 more than I was making. Back in 1973, three grand, as my Uncle Mario would often say, "ain't tinsel."

After praying for a little help with the decision-making process, I took the offer.

My first day on the new job was a day to remember. That morning, Bud decided to show me the main warehouse at the corner of 15th and Sydenham Streets. When we rode the large freight elevator to the third floor, I was impressed with all of the furniture and equipment that was neatly stored. As Bud walked over to a wall phone to call the office, I noticed a piano alongside a rectangular, wooden railing. I decided to go over and test how the piano sounded. It was clear that it was a shorter trip if I walked in between the wooden rails, instead of walking around the structure. I did so and reached out to touch the keys. The next thing I knew, I was holding onto one of the rails with one hand, dangling three floors up over a large opening that contained the hoist used to lift the heavy equipment. Obviously, my guardian angel had decided to visit the warehouse too. I don't remember grabbing the rail. Later, I kidded Bud that I had decided to make my new boss a hero on day one, which he became when he rushed over and pulled me up to safety.

Bud and I had adjoining offices. His was to the side of mine, which was next to the corridor that was clearly visible through the large, glass window. One afternoon, as I sat at my desk talking with Bud, I happened to glance up and, through the window, I saw a beautiful young lady walk by on her way to the copy machine. I had never seen her before, and the way she looked in her pink slacks only reinforced my steadfast belief that God knew what He was doing.

"Yo, Bud," I asked, "Who is that?"

"Oh, that's Rose's daughter." Rose was a lovely lady who worked in our payroll department.

"I have to introduce myself."

Now, I was the youngest manager in the entire department. Most guys were in their 40s and 50s. I was 25. I didn't want people to think that I was just there to meet coeds, so I picked up a document to take to the copier. While at the machine, I introduced myself to Rose's daughter, and I learned that her name was Luann. We spoke for about 10 minutes and, when we were through, I had a date to play tennis with her on that Saturday. Luann was 18. As I said earlier, I was 25. In case you are unfamiliar with the Sicilian-American culture, let's just say that there was no way I could ever get near her, given our age difference, if Rose didn't know me and vouch for me with Fred, her strict, Sicilian husband.

That Saturday, it rained like mad. Undeterred, I went over to Luann's house anyway, and Fred answered the door. We shook hands, and I knew I had hit the jackpot when the fresh aroma of fried, stuffed peppers filled the air. It was a great visit, and I was treated with typical Italian hospitality.

Back in 1973, I was pretty impressed with myself after arranging that first date so quickly, at the copy machine, although the planned activity for the day didn't materialize due to the inclement weather. But I surely can't complain after the way things worked out. By the way, after two years of courtship and 43 years of marriage, we still haven't hit that tennis ball.

Mary's Garden at The Church of the Sacred Heart

8

Keeping "In Touch"

ON JUNE 26TH, 1979, my wife, Luann, and I were blessed with the birth of our first child: a beautiful, little daughter. For me, it was an extra kick because it happened to be my birthday. Naturally, everyone in the family was thrilled with our new addition. She would have four loving grandparents to dote over her and shower her with a ton of love. My parents already had two granddaughters, from my sister and her husband, so the birth of our daughter was extra special for my wife's parents, Fred and Rose, who now had their first grandchild.

Rose was a sweet, loving lady who exuded femininity in the fairest sense of the word. She was the ideal mother-in-law, never butting into our affairs yet always there if asked for advice. I joked while delivering her eulogy that the only bone I had to pick with her was that she had prevented me from telling "mother-in-law" jokes because she was so nice. My father-in-law was a handsome, hard-working, gregarious man whose chief loves in life were God, family, and Sinatra ... Perhaps not always in that order! He was quite the kidder too. Like her mother, my wife is a meticulous housekeeper, but that might surprise anyone who knew her as a child. Little Luann was a holy terror, grabbing everything in sight, knocking things over, jumping on furniture, sliding down the banister, and just generally getting into mischief.

Dad saw his opportunity for a little good-natured "payback." Just about as soon as our daughter was born, he stated his intention to teach her how to run around the house and grab the tablecloth, throw newspapers, and perform other feats of mayhem. At her 1st birthday party, Dad was true to form. He produced a neatly wrapped present and, upon opening it, we discovered a very realistic-looking toy hammer. He was quick to point out that it would be put to good use once he was able to teach the baby how to wield it.

Three years later, on December 19th, our son came along. My wife's pregnancy was a very emotional one because, at the time, her Dad was engaged in a very courageous battle with lung cancer. Dad died just two months before our son's birth, so the new arrival was greeted with emotions of every type. Like many great mothers, Rose came to our house in Drexel Hill, Pennsylvania, to assist the new mom while she was getting back on her feet. After a few days, it was time to take Mom back home to New Jersey. Earlier that morning, I decided to take a walk to the shopping center to pick up a few things. The half-mile walk gave me time to reflect upon the events of the last week and take stock of my new responsibilities as a father of two. As I walked down State Road towards Lansdowne Avenue, I thought of Fred and said a quick prayer, thinking, "Boy, Dad, too bad you're not around. Now you have a grandson who could really make use of a hammer."

A few hours later, I loaded up the car with Mom's things to take her home. We started our trip and, after about a mile, I drove up the hill just past Garrett Road. In the distance, I saw a fairly large object in the street, which I would have to avoid. As I approached it, my heart skipped a beat, and I let out an audible "Whoa," startling Mom. There, in the middle of the road, was a brand-new, shiny *hammer*. Not a plastic, toy one; a real one, like the kind all men keep in their toolboxes! I kept driving, adrenaline pumping, and told Mom the whole story, from my walk to the store up to that very moment. She looked at me in amazement.

Was the hammer in the street a coincidence? I've been driving for over 50 years, and I've never seen a hammer in the road. I have unfortunately met up with a nail or two, but never a brand-new hammer. Naturally, this story was shared with the entire family the day it occurred and many times thereafter.

Fast-forward 24 years. That baby boy is now a young man contemplating a proposal of marriage to the love of his life. Although sure this is the right thing to do, he has the normal amount of anxiety as he realizes how his life will change forever. Still, the big day arrived, and he would pop the question after Sunday mass at the Church of the Sacred Heart in Riverton, New Jersey, which incidentally was the site where my wife and I tied the knot. After mass, the young couple strolled into "Mary's Garden," a scenic shrine dedicated to the Blessed Mother. My son's nervousness immediately disappeared when he looked at a nearby bench and saw a shiny *hammer* just sitting there. He then realized that his "Pop-Pop" was giving him the message: "Go for it, kid, and don't worry about a thing."

As for me, I have chosen to believe that those hammers were clear examples of Dad's sense of humor. Symbols which let us know that, even though he isn't down here with us, he is still looking out for us and loving his family.

9

A Gift of Mercy

OCTOBER 3RD, 1988, was a very long day for my mother, Catherine, and me. We had arrived at Fitzgerald Mercy Hospital in Darby, Pennsylvania, at 6:00 a.m. We would not leave until 16 hours later. The reason we were there was to lend support to my father, Henry, who would be undergoing surgery to remove a cancerous prostate gland. Multiple emergencies and other delays caused the surgery, originally scheduled for 8:00 a.m., to commence at 6:00 p.m. By the time Dad had awakened and had been taken to his room, it was 9:00 p.m. We stayed with our groggy loved one until 10:00, when sheer exhaustion from the long hours of frustration, worry, and stress won out, then we waved the white flag of surrender and left for home. We were beat, especially Mom, who was 80 years old at the time.

To say that I was in a hurry to get Mom home and hit the sack in my own bed in New Jersey would be an understatement. As we left the parking garage in my 1978 Malibu Classic, I made a quick turn onto Lansdowne Avenue and took off. By the time I made the short ride to the intersection at MacDade Boulevard, I saw the flashing red-and-blue lights in my rear-view mirror. After pulling over, I rolled down the window to speak with the police officer, who told me I was doing 40 in a 25-mph zone. His tone was nearly jubilant, but I was in no mood to dispute him, so I simply took the ticket and drove (carefully) away. I had been caught in a speed trap with no visible speed-limit sign displayed from my departure point to where I was stopped.

The ticket was for $120, which I was ready to pay and forget about until I was reminded that a moving violation would earn me a three-year "surcharge" on my insurance premium, most likely totaling about $300 per year. Now we had a different ballgame. I decided to go to court and plead my case. I received the summons and, in three weeks, I would have my day in court. That morning, the courtroom was very crowded, and I found out I would be the fifth case heard. I recognized the cop who had given me the ticket when he entered and took his place at a podium to the right of the judge's bench. I realized that this guy was very familiar with the process and was probably one of Darby's largest fundraisers. This particular speed trap was apparently his little gold mine. I felt it wise to observe how the judge handled himself as he heard the various excuses. Perhaps this would give me the edge I needed to avoid the $1,000 payoff for which I was on the hook.

As I sat waiting for the first case to be heard, I reached into my pocket to be sure I had the letter I retrieved from the surgeon, which stated that Dad's surgery had been delayed and that Mom and I had spent 16 hours at the hospital. The first defendant was caught in the speed trap doing 42 mph. A man of about 30 years of age, he told the judge he was from out of town and wasn't familiar with the area. Nice try, buddy.

"Guilty! Fine and costs ... See the clerk!"

I wasn't about to use that excuse. The next case involved two elderly ladies who entered the trap and were doing 40 mph, like me. They said they were driving home from a Bible-study class and, while discussing the teachings, didn't realize how fast they were going. They were so sweet that I was tempted to go and pay their fine, but it wasn't necessary.

"Case dismissed. Please drive more carefully, ladies!" The cop didn't look too happy.

That excuse also wouldn't work for me. They were much more lovable than I was. The next case was an attractive young lady in her twenties who said she was blinded by the sun glare and, therefore, never saw a speed-limit sign. Unfortunately, she didn't take the time to read her ticket, which the cop was very eager to point out listed the weather conditions as "rainy."

"Guilty! Fine and costs ... See the clerk!"

The next guy thought the better of it and just plead guilty. The judge showed his gratitude:

"Guilty! Court costs waived ... See the clerk!" At least the motorist saved about 20 bucks. He walked out, acting as though he had hit the lottery.

Now it was my turn. From observing the previous four cases, I determined that the judge was no fool and was capable of showing compassion if he sensed sincerity. I'd give it my best shot. When the judge asked me to present my case, I said a silent prayer for the Holy Spirit's guidance. Then I faced the judge and said:

"Your Honor, I am not disputing the officer's assertion that I drove over the speed limit. I was very tired and under a lot of stress, since my 80-year-old mother and I had spent 16 hours at the hospital, as my father was undergoing cancer surgery. I just wanted to take her home to get some rest and then get back to my home, which is 40 miles away. I meant no disrespect to the law and have never had a moving violation in the 40-plus years I've been driving. Also, Your Honor, I happen to have a letter from the surgeon attesting to the fact that we had such a long, stressful day, just in case you'd like to read it."

The judge asked for the letter, looked at me for a few seconds, then looked at the cop and said, "You know, officer, it's obvious that sometimes the stress of such a trying day as this can cause a good citizen to make an honest mistake.

"Case dismissed. Have a safe trip home!" As I left the courtroom, I gave the cop a smile, and he gave me one too.

By the way, Dad did fine, lived another 16 good years, and when I hear the name Fitzgerald *Mercy* Hospital, I think about the little bit of mercy thrown my way back in 1988.

10

The Angelic Backup

Livingston County Testing Service

IN THE SUMMER of 1996, my wife, Luann, and I prepared for one of the most stressful events any parent has to endure. Our daughter, Rosanne, had reached the age that the state of New Jersey believed was appropriate to offer her a driver's permit. As far as I was concerned, I would have preferred that day to be about 10 years down the road, but Rosie would have none of that. Having been genetically "blessed" with both impatience and persistence, she felt that she could surely outlast us. Naturally, she was right, and we enrolled her in a local driving school for a six-week course. I must say that she did remarkably well, as far as actual driving was concerned. Her problem was the same as many New Jersey kids: the inability to parallel park.

For guys like me who grew up in Philadelphia, parallel parking was a skill handed down from generation to generation. You had to learn to park in the city because very few people had driveways and garages. It's just the opposite where we live in Jersey. Hardly anyone needs to parallel park, in tight spots, because almost every home has a driveway or garage. Rosie just couldn't get the hang of it. If she didn't turn the wheel the wrong way, then she made some other mistake, like end up two feet from the curb. When the day came for her to go with her teacher to take the driving test, the results were unfortunately predictable: Flunksville. The reason? "Inability to parallel park."

Somewhat depressed, Rosie elicited her mom's assistance to smooth out the rough spots in her parking technique. The only problem was that Luann is also a product of New Jersey, so she can't parallel park either. Therefore, her sincere two weeks of work with Rosie were to no avail. It seemed highly likely that Rosie was headed for trouble when her September retest date arrived.

It became apparent that I was Rosie's last, best chance. My family always marveled at my ability to back into the tightest of spaces when we would visit relatives in Philly. I always considered parallel parking to be akin to twirling spaghetti with a fork and spoon. It might be hard to master, but once you do, you never forget. Although I was Rosie's second choice in the teacher pecking order, she knew that she needed help. Time was wasting. So I gathered up four milk crates, and we drove to a nearby street in an industrial park to set up the "practice field," so to speak. I had driven to the local testing center and measured the rectangular parallel parking test area. I set up the crates to spec, placing two of them alongside the actual curb and the other two further out, forming the allowable parking zone. I sat in the car with Rosie and explained the parking technique that had served me well on so many of those city streets. She listened attentively, and then it was time to put all of my sage instruction into action. She pulled up alongside the imaginary test area and started to back up.

BANG!

She had turned the wheel the wrong way, and her right front tire smashed the left front milk crate. Undaunted, we tried once more.

SCRAAATCH!

She backed in ok but jumped the curb after scraping the sidewall. Several more sessions proved fruitless and, the next thing we knew, the day of the test had arrived.

While driving Rosie to the testing facility, I felt it was time for a reality check. I said, "Ro, let's face it: There is no way you can pass the parking part of this test. What I think you should do is say a prayer, and ask God to let your guardian angel take over the wheel when you park. That's your only shot."

Tough love!

I also found out that Luann had placed a small statue of the Blessed Mother on the back seat, wrapped in a towel. This brought the concept of the "backseat driver" to a new level.

When we arrived, we were greeted by the guy who would administer the test. He looked like he didn't want to be there. I noticed that he was wearing a Yankees cap, so I tried to loosen him up by talking a little baseball and mentioning how much I admired Derek Jeter. No reaction. As I was walking toward the sidewalk, I looked over my shoulder to see Rosie pull away for the driving part of the exam. No problem, she handled the car beautifully. Now it was time to park. The suspense was killing me. I stood behind a large bush and, through squinting eyes, watched as my little girl parked the car with only one backup, stopping six inches from the curb. Perfect.

She passed!

You might say that it was just luck or that the law of averages came into play. But, as far as Rosie and I are concerned, we know who really parked the car that day.

11

An Unlikely Messenger

I'LL NEVER FORGET what happened to me on my 50th birthday. I say this not because of a big surprise party or other event marking what many feel to be a milestone. Instead, something happened to me that may be the most spiritual experience I've ever had, and it came from a rather unlikely source.

In 1997, I was well into my sales career, and there was a lot going on in my life. I had two children, one in college and one in high school, and a stay-at-home wife whose job was to take care of all three of us and who did her job very well. I was working as a straight-commission salesman, which meant that, each time I left my home to drive to my territory, I had no idea as to how much money, if any, I would earn that day. Being a commissioned salesman can be either motivating or devastating. You have to sell to earn a paycheck. If you don't sell, your family is in jeopardy. The everyday pressure of that reality was something I had to live with and handle. At this particular time of my life, I was feeling a bit uneasy. It was summer, and I was having back problems. Carrying that heavy sample case didn't make my back pain feel any better. I'd have to admit that a bunch of stuff was starting to pile up, and I wasn't in the best frame of mind. As a spiritual person, I have always trusted in God to take care of all of us but I, like most human beings, have my weaker moments.

As I left our home in New Jersey to drive to my destination for the day, which was the Pottstown, Pennsylvania, area, I would have plenty of time to think. The 50-mile commute was usually unpleasant. It involved driving on I-95, the Schuylkill Expressway, and Route 422 West. I-95 and the expressway were always full of surprises, usually bad ones, and 422 was very heavily traveled. The impending driving drudgery aside, I did have a spark of happy anticipation. Since this day, June 26th, 1997, was my 50th birthday, I was looking forward to my return home and my quiet celebration with my family. As my commute began, I quickly encountered a traffic jam on I-95, just a short distance from my home. The knowledge that this would make a long trip even longer caused me to forget about any birthday joy, as my day would begin with a good measure of aggravation.

The extended commute would last about two hours, and as I slowly (and I mean *slowly*) negotiated the expressway and then picked up 422 near King of Prussia, my case of the "blahs" was a steady companion. Even the music playing on my radio didn't do much to put me in a good frame of mind. As I exited 422 at Hanover Street in Pottstown, something happened that served not only to lighten my heart but to bring me inner peace in a most profound way.

I HEARD ROD STEWART'S SOULFUL RENDITION OF A SONG COMPOSED BY VAN MORRISON:

Have I Told You Lately That I Love You?

It was playing very loudly, although I hadn't turned up the volume. I was never a huge Rod Stewart fan but, somehow, as I drove toward High Street, my mind intently focused on the lyrics:

Have I told you lately that I love you?
Have I told you there's no one above you?
Fill my heart with gladness,
Take away all my sadness,
Ease my troubles, that's what you do.

Oh, the morning sun with all its glory
Greets the day with hope and comfort too.
And you fill my life with laughter.
You can make it better.
Ease my troubles, that's what you do.
There's a love that's divine,
And it's yours and mine,

Like the sun.
At the end of the day,
We should give thanks and pray to the One, to the One.

This was a beautiful love song. But for me, at that moment, it wasn't about love between a man and a woman. It was about how God loves us. As I digested those lyrics with that in mind, the fog that enveloped me was lifted, and I immediately felt like my old self. It was a wonderful renewal of what I have always believed: that Our Lord will continue to take care of us, even in our weakest moments.

I have heard that song countless times over the years. Each time I do, it lifts me up, and it's a blessing.

12

Watching My Back

St. Michael the Archangel

WHEN YOU'RE ON earth for more than seven decades, you realize that you can relax a little. You don't have to worry about a lot of the things that concerned you when you were younger and in a different stage of life. For instance, when I was a young man, I'd never wear white socks with shoes and slacks. The socks were always black or brown. Now, who cares? Years ago, I may have had concerns about what others thought when I brought up a somewhat controversial topic. Now, I rarely do, which leads me to the issue at hand: I have total faith in the fact that I do have a guardian angel who has been tasked with looking out for me. I realize that not all will agree but, in my case, I have had one too many close calls, and angelic intervention no doubt has played a big part in my weathering those storms.

For instance, when I was 26, back in 1973, it was the first day of my new job in Temple University's Facilities Department. My new boss, Bud Wilson, decided to show me the central warehouse at the corner of 15th and Sydenham Streets on the main campus. This was a good idea because the distribution of the furniture stored there was one of our areas of responsibility. When we rode the large freight elevator to the third floor, I was impressed with all of the neatly stored furniture and equipment. As Bud walked over to a wall phone to call the office, I noticed a piano alongside a rectangular, wooden railing. I decided to go over and test how the piano sounded. It was clear that it was a shorter trip if I walked in between the wooden rails, instead of walking around the structure. I did so and reached out to touch the keys. The next thing I knew, I was holding onto one of the rails with one hand, dangling three floors up over a large opening that contained the hoist used to lift heavy loads. I don't remember grabbing the rail. Bud was a hero as he pulled me up to safety but, after I thought about it, I realized that grabbing that railing, in that split second, was something I had never thought of doing.

Five years earlier, I was playing baseball in a college league in South Dakota. Since the teams included ballplayers from all over the country, I enjoyed the opportunity to make new friends and compete with some very talented guys. Among my teammates were three guys from California. Our games were played at night, so on a very hot afternoon, the guys decided to go "tubing" on a local river. As a kid, our Philadelphia neighborhood "swim club" was located at the 64th Street fire hydrant. Since the water didn't get more than two inches deep, I never learned to swim a stroke! So when the guys asked me to go along on the tubing trip, I declined. However, after many assurances that the water in the river was shallow, and we'd all be together, I decided to take the plunge, so to speak. This was not one of my wisest decisions. Two guys had cars. One parked about two miles downstream, and then we all drove upstream to the launching point. As I held my inner tube, I noticed that the current was pretty strong, and thought perhaps I made the wrong call. However, I jumped on the tube and started to be whisked away. In a matter of seconds, I realized that the water was a lot deeper than advertised, I had no control over the steering, and those guys were way downstream, so I was on my own.

I jumped off.

Clinging to the tube, I barely made it back to the shore. Sitting down to catch my breath, I realized that I could easily have been one of those drowning victims that we, unfortunately, hear about every summer. I was thankful that, somehow, I was brought to my senses, and I was now safe. As I walked back to the car, I was attacked by hordes of mosquitoes. The car was locked. With only a bathing suit to protect me, I became an Italian smorgasbord for about an hour and a half, until the others returned.

The incident that really convinced me of my angelic intervention occurred in the winter of 2002. On this day, I had been working in the Princeton, New Jersey, area, about 35 miles from my home. I was running on very little sleep and fighting off a terrible cold. This had proven to be a very long day and, as I headed south on a dark Interstate 295, I was really feeling drowsy. It was well after rush hour, so the traffic was moving at the rate of 70 to 75 mph. I fe t myself nodding off but was able to shake it by opening the window, raising the volume of the radio, and making a conscious effort to focus on the details of my surroundings. I noticed that I was approaching **Exit 47B, the Burlington-Mt. Holly**. I thought, "Great! I only have about 10 miles to go."

That's the last thing I remembered until I opened my eyes and saw the sign that read: **Exit 40, Moorestown**.

I am convinced that I was not in control of the car for those 10 miles. I was not awake. I passed five exits and then awoke just in time to get off at my exit and arrive safely home.

As I sit at my desk typing this, I can look up and see my five-inch statues of the Archangels: Michael, Gabriel, and Raphael. I can't be sure that any of *these* guys were with me on those days of near disaster, but I am certain that one or two of their buddies were.

13

No Harm in Asking

Our Lady of Loreto Church

MY FATHER, HENRY, paid a price for working at the Westinghouse plant in Lester, Pennsylvania, for 40-plus years.

The constant pounding of his drop forge hammer had caused him to lose most of his hearing. He was "old school" and happy to have this job that kept my mother and him fed and warm during their 65-year marriage. Suing the company was out of the question for a man like him. He knew the risks, and that was that. My mother, sister, and I got used to having to elevate our voices when we spoke with Dad. We also got used to the TV blaring at night and, every summer, my Buist Avenue neighbors enjoyed the free radio broadcasts of every Phillies game that emanated from the open windows. My dear friend, Tom Manieri, who was a member of the wonderful service organization the Lion's Club, used his influence to provide Dad with two free hearing aids. The only problem was that Dad didn't like them, so he rarely used them. Also, as is typical with most hard-of-hearing people, he tended to speak in a very loud voice so that he could hear himself!

As he grew older, he developed some health problems. He became an insulin-dependent diabetic. Well into his 80s and a widower after Mom's death, he valued his independence and was quite self-sufficient. He was still driving at age 87. I kept close tabs on him and came to realize that the effects of his diabetes were becoming dangerous. We had discussed the possibility of giving up his car, which he staunchly resisted.

Until one night.

At the dinner table, his sugar level dropped, and he was "out of it" for about 20 seconds. After I said that being out of control for that long while driving could possibly cause an accident that might result in an innocent kid's death, right then and there, he agreed to stop driving. I took the keys, gave them to my cousin, and Dad's driving days were over. It became my responsibility to take him wherever he had to go, whether it was to the store, to the doctor's, to visit his sister and, yes, even to church every Sunday, unless one of my nieces, his granddaughters, Catrese or Kristina, paid a visit. I didn't mind. It gave us a chance to get together and talk about family and baseball, his two favorite topics.

Dad and Mom belonged to Our Lady of Loreto church, located at the corner of 62nd Street and Grays Avenue in southwest Philly. This was one of the old, ethnic parishes, and the parishioners were mostly Italian-Americans. My parents had been fixtures at the eight o'clock mass every Sunday for over 50 years, occupying the same seats in the second row, just to the right of the speaker's podium. With Mom gone, I would pick up Dad, sit in those same seats, and since no one sat in the front row, we were the closest parishioners to the priest.

Dad was now 90 years old and, on one particular Sunday, we had a young visiting priest. He was sent by the bishop to share his experiences from his six months of studies in Rome. As the guest started to give his remarks, our pastor took his seat just to our left. Our guest was an enthusiastic young man, but to say that he was a bit "wordy" would be an understatement. First, he spoke for a few minutes on the overall beauty of Rome. He then gave his impressions of Vatican City, which included a 10-minute description of the Sistine Chapel that the most seasoned tour guide would envy. This was followed by another 10 minutes or so of his thoughts on St. Peter's Basilica, the Coliseum, and the Appian Way. I felt as though I'd soon be hearing the banging of heads on the wooden pews as the congregation dozed off, one by one. Remarkably, my father just sat there, wide awake, watching the young man speak. Suddenly, he turned to me and said in a very audible voice:

"What's this guy talking about?"

Our guest's eyes opened wide. I looked for a place to hide but, alas, there was none. Our pastor smiled, perhaps giving tacit approval. Dad just sat there, his question unanswered.

As we filed out after mass, a couple of the old, Italian guys in the congregation came up to us and patted Dad on the back. One man said he wished he had asked that question. Dad didn't mean to be disrespectful. He would never do that. However, I think his easily overheard question was an example of how God works in strange ways, and it served two purposes. First, the young priest must have realized he had gone on too long and was losing his audience. He ended his talk soon after hearing Dad's question. Second, perhaps the young priest learned a lesson in brevity and, hopefully, this would help him in the years to come as he tended to his own flock.

14

A Match Made in Heaven

Sister Mary Ann and the Author

I MADE A wonderful friend back in the summer of 2003, and there can be no doubt that it was the result of Divine Intervention. The interesting thing about the start of this friendship is that it occurred in the most unlikely of places … Atlantic City, New Jersey, the gambling capital of the east.

On a sunny Saturday in August, I took my wife and daughter to Atlantic City so that they could enjoy a few hours of shopping at the newly opened Tanger Outlets on Baltic Avenue. Since I consider shopping with one or both of my girls similar to my upcoming stint in Purgatory, I decided to let them go shopping without me while I would take a stroll on the famous "Boardwalk" and perhaps try my luck at a casino or two. We agreed to meet at a specific location in three hours, and off we went. Later, as I glanced at my watch, I realized our 4:00 p.m. rendezvous time was near. I also remembered that there was a Saturday-evening mass at the local Catholic Church, Our Lady Star of the Sea. Since mass would begin in a short while, this would be a convenient opportunity for us to fulfill our weekly obligation by attending the service. While inside the church, waiting for the mass to begin, I started reading the weekly bulletin. I noticed a school "Wish List," and it aroused my curiosity.

The list represented some items which were greatly needed but deemed to be too costly to supply in adequate numbers. It included items like pencil sharpeners, CD players, DVD players, etc. Since these items were typical, basic ones that every school usually has, it was obvious that this school must need assistance, so I followed the instructions for those who wanted to help. I contacted Sister Mary Ann, a member of the Sisters of Mercy order of nuns, who was the school guidance counselor and Jack-of-all-trades (or should I say, "Jill"?). Our phone conversation sparked what has become a wonderful relationship.

I learned that the school opened in 1908. The grades taught were Pre-K to eighth and, since the school was established by the parish, the parish alone was responsible for funding the school. In its heyday, the school was educating about 400 students. Since Atlantic City has been hurting economically (most of the students' parents work at the casinos), and due to the general poverty of the families involved, the school's enrollment numbers have decreased significantly. It is now the only Catholic school operating in Atlantic City and all of Absecon Island. Tuition is established and based on the average family income, taking into account the financial plight of the families. Among the services provided to the students, the school has breakfast, hot lunch, and after-care programs at a nominal charge, and these are managed by volunteers. The students have come from countries all over the world, including China, Vietnam, Bangladesh, India, Mexico, Colombia, Argentina, Puerto Rico, Pakistan, the Philippines, and, of course, the USA. It is common for the foreign children to greatly improve their English language skills just through their contact with the American kids. Sister Mary Ann shared some student success stories with me, including a U.S. Naval Academy student, a Ph.D., and an M.D.

As our relationship developed, I discovered that Sister Mary Ann was a Philly girl. As a kid, she was the ultimate "tomboy" who played baseball with all of the boys in the neighborhood and held her own. Like my daughter, she is a die-hard Phillies fan who cheers with every victory and hurts with every loss.

My kind of girl!

One of the things that has touched me the most is the absolute joy the kids show as they attend school. They are well-behaved, happy children, and it is obvious that this school is just about the best thing they have going on in their lives. Over the years, being blessed with generous friends and wonderful customers, I have been privileged to coordinate donations to the school, both of a monetary and material nature. I will never forget the time that I delivered several large trash bags filled with used soccer balls, basketballs, and footballs donated by my friend who works at a school in Pennsylvania. When the group of third-graders saw the balls, you would have thought they had discovered a pot of gold. A lot of kids wouldn't even want to play with anything "used," but these kids truly appreciated the charity and kindness shown to them. Their smiles and laughter made me realize how blessed I was to see it all.

If you had told me 15 years ago that, among the friends that I would hold dearly, there would be an ex-principal, Phillies-loving nun from northeast Philly who now counsels poor kids from all over the world at an Atlantic City school, I may have accused you of staying too long at Happy Hour.

I think I'll just chalk it up to Divine Providence.

15

His Way

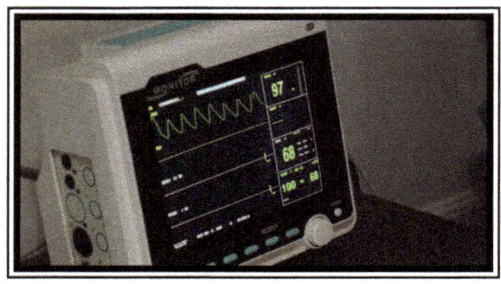

BY NECESSITY, WHILE recuperating from extensive knee surgery for eight weeks in 2018, I had to become more and more dependent on my wife, Luann, to do things for me. Not being able to easily move around will do that to you. Whether it involved getting me a bottle of water, going up and down the stairs every time I had a meal, putting on my socks or catering to any other of my whims, my wife served in the most loving way. Recuperation also provided me with a lot of time to think. I remember, during my hospital stay, my thoughts drifted to my father Henry's last days, as he spent them hospitalized. His short stay, however, was much more eventful than mine.

Having been a widower for two years after our Mom

Catherine's death in May of 2002, Dad, at age 91, fought to stay independent, living in Philadelphia in that big Buist Avenue row home, alone. He drove, shopped, walked to the bank, made house repairs, and generally worried us to death. One vivid memory I have is driving down his street for a visit and seeing Dad, then 89, climbing down from the top of his upper roof after repairing a leak. Earlier, he had climbed out of his bedroom window onto the lower roof, leaned the ladder against the wall, and climbed to the top.

This was a tough guy.

Being that Dad was this way, one can understand his absolute unwillingness to become a burden to his children. However, no one can beat the aging process and, sooner or later, even the toughest of men face that reality. In Dad's case, his diabetes and heart condition had started to take their tolls. I brought up the idea of his moving in with us, but that suggestion didn't fly. Only after his sugar issues caused him to have brief, near-blackout episodes did he consent to end his driving. Recognizing the opportunity, I simply told him that these episodes could put an innocent child at risk, which was all I had to say. I became his chauffeur. The shortness of breath occurred more frequently too. At the age of 91, he caught a terrible cold and, after I took him to his doctor, he was admitted to Mercy Catholic Hospital. Dad was diagnosed with congestive heart failure and, after two days, we laid down the law and told him that the "jig was up," and he'd be living with us from then on. He didn't argue this time.

The plan was for Dad to stay with my sister, Kathy, and her husband, George, for a few days to give us time to make all of the logistical arrangements for his move-in, so off he went to Kathy's house in New Jersey. However, two days later, he had another bout with heart failure and was admitted to Virtua Hospital in Voorhees. This was not a good visit. Dad wanted out and had to be restrained at one point to prevent him from sneaking down the fire escape. When I visited him, he told me to untie the straps holding his arms to the bed. I said, "Not if you're going to try to fly the coop!" He promised he'd behave, so I told the nurses to undo the restraints. He calmed down.

The next night was Friday, the 15th of October. My wife and I, along with our daughter Rosie, went to visit. Rosie gave Dad a beautiful holy card of the Blessed Mother and tacked it onto the bulletin board so he could see it from his bed. Our son was studying for an exam and intended to visit the next day. Dad looked remarkably well. He was sitting up in bed and having a ball talking to an African-American nurse who happened to speak fluent Italian. I wished that we had an interpreter since their conversation was full of laughs, and we could only enjoy the moment from afar. After the nurse left, Dad took better notice of the holy card and asked to see it.

What followed was amazing to us.

Dad took the card, kissed it, and then looked into space with the most peaceful, angelic smile I had ever seen. I immediately thought that he had a vision of his loving wife, whose devotion to our Blessed Mary was complete and endless. All three of us were awestruck by this expression on his face that none of us had ever witnessed.

When he was finished with the card, Rosie reattached it to the board. I then told Dad that his grandson was studying and would come back with me tomorrow to see him. Dad, relaxed and lucid, simply said:

"I'm not gonna be here tomorrow."

I said, "Dad, don't start that stuff again, you aren't going anywhere until they release you." Soon after, visiting hours were over, and it was time to leave. At 8:00 p.m., we left for home after kissing Dad goodbye.

At 6:00 the next morning, Saturday, October 16th, I received a call from Dad's cardiologist, who told me that Dad had passed away peacefully at 2:00 a.m. Ironically, Dad had died on the same day, October 16th, that Luann's Dad had died many years earlier.

Dad had done it his way. He wasn't going to be a burden, and he sure wasn't going to "**be there tomorrow**."

God had other plans.

16

An Enduring Gift

Mom's Statue on its Display Stand

MOM'S STATUE HAS been part of our family for over 40 years. The story about how this came to be is both interesting and fateful.

In 1972, I was a member of the 103rd Engineer Battalion of the Pennsylvania National Guard. As part of our training, we

were required to complete two weeks of summer "field" training, usually at an Army facility. That year, we were scheduled
to commence training at Camp Drum, New York, in June.

On June 16th, 1972, something happened to change our
plans ... the arrival of Hurricane Agnes. Causing wide-
spread havoc, Agnes took particular aim on the Wilkes-Barre,
Pennsylvania, area. Our unit was redeployed to help clean up
in her aftermath.

I was to act as the chaplain's driver. It was my job to transport
our chaplain, a Catholic priest, around the area to lend spiritual comfort to those who had lost everything. Homes were
leveled by the force of the water. The Susquehanna River rose
to rooftop heights, destroying everything in its path. Coffins
littered the streets, deposited after the gravesites were eroded
by the water flow. Shopping center parking lots were now
lakes. The streets were covered with mud, the sediment of the
receding water. Drying mud became dust. We needed surgi-
cal masks to breathe properly. These scenes were surreal.

One morning, I drove Father to an officers' meeting. Since I
had about an hour of free time while he attended the meeting, I decided to do some sightseeing. On a residential street, I
saw nothing but rubble, the remains of some beautiful homes.
The residents had apparently scavenged through the debris
because some of the rubble was in piles, small and large. To
my left, I saw a large pile, five feet high by eight feet long.
From a distance, I could see a small object on top that looked
somewhat out of place. As I drove closer, I realized it was a
3 ½-inch statue of Mary, the Blessed Mother. I felt a sense of
wonder and love as I realized the message God was sending

me. He was telling me that He and his Mother would always be with me, even in the most horrendous situations. I stopped the Jeep, walked over, picked up the statue and, after a kiss of respect, I put it in the pocket of my fatigue pants.

Upon my arrival home, I presented the statue to my mother, Catherine. She was devoted to Our Lady and prayed to her every day. After telling Mom the whole story, she placed the statue on the windowsill of her kitchen. As an avid cook, she spent much of the next 30 years with her statue. Indeed, when Mom had her stroke on April 26th, 2002, four days after her 94th birthday, she was in her kitchen.

Mom was rushed to the hospital that day and stayed there until she died on May 11th, 2002. I brought the statue to the hospital and, although Mom never regained full consciousness, she held that statue tightly during her entire stay ... except for one night. As we visited, my sister, Kathy, and I noticed that the statue wasn't in Mom's hand. We had seen it earlier that day, so the disappearance was very mysterious. We looked in the bed, throughout the room, and questioned the personnel. There was no sign of the beloved statue. I joked that Our Lady had taken a quick trip to heaven to prepare Mom's room! Upon leaving, I knew that somehow the Blessed Lady would be back in the morning. The next day, there she was all right, back in Mom's hand, a true mystery. None of the hospital personnel had an explanation. Mom held her until the day she died. In Mom's last moments of life, when she was very weak and barely breathing, her grip on the statue was so powerful, I couldn't remove it. At the viewing, Mom was lying in state, and I placed the statue on her right shoulder. Both ladies looked very peaceful.

I told the story to a customer who suggested that one of his carpenters would fabricate a stand so that the statue could be displayed in a nice setting. He recommended that it include a little pocket in which I could store this letter for all to read.

For all of you who read this, rest assured that our family has been blessed by God above, and Mom's statue of the Blessed Mother was, and is, a remembrance of Mom and her devotion to the Mother of God.

17

Mary, Tony, and the Midnight Visitor

Tony and Mary Rocca

IN NOVEMBER OF 2008, like many elderly south Philadelphia residents, our Aunt Mary and Uncle Tony Rocca enjoyed taking the late-afternoon bus ride to the casino in Atlantic City. Certainly, at the age of 88, they both deserved to have a little fun after raising their three kids in a most selfless and devoted way. Uncle Tony learned the printing business as a young apprentice and was able to start his own successful company over 60 years earlier. Aunt Mary was the typical Italian housewife, taking care of her kids and home while squeezing in daily mass at the Epiphany of Our Lord Roman Catholic Church, only a few blocks away from their Wolf Street home.

Her piousness was well known in the neighborhood. Each day she would buy a fresh loaf of Italian bread at the bakery down the street. Since she arrived there at various times, the baker always put a loaf aside for her. On the bag, he would mark, "Holy Mary," so everyone knew to whom it belonged. Although Uncle Tony had turned over the day-to-day operation of the business to his sons, Bob and Tony, the big guy still made regular appearances, just to be sure things were going well. By 2008, Uncle Tony had an array of physical issues, including the inability to walk without the use of a cane, due to his two damaged knees. However, he gladly endured that discomfort to make sure his beloved wife of 64 years had the opportunity to drop her quarters into the slots at the Showboat Casino.

This above-mentioned trip was coming to an end, and the bus was just about ready to leave for home. Mary was finished playing and sat on one of the elevated seats at a nearby, vacant blackjack table, while Tony attempted to get a few more pulls on the "one-armed bandit." When Tony finally surrendered, Mary began to get out of the seat. In doing so, she lost her balance and fell abruptly onto the floor. As she writhed in pain, Tony made a valiant effort to help her. Two security guards came to Mary's aid almost immediately and offered to take her to the local hospital. Mary resisted and instead waived her right to medical attention. She requested to be taken to the bus for the ride home, and her wish was granted.

As the trip progressed, Mary's pain in the abdominal area worsened. Upon their arrival in Philly, Mary and Tony were let off the bus only a short distance from their home. The bus driver obviously altered his route to do so, then made a hasty departure. It took them a while to exit the bus, and then they were alone. Mary was unable to walk. Due to his condition, Tony was unable to help her negotiate the short distance to the house. They were faced with the realization that they were out on the streets of Philadelphia, alone, at 12:30 a.m. They were 88 years old, Mary was injured, in excruciating pain, and it seemed a sure thing that they would be unable to get to their destination. They were easy prey for any bad guy who was looking for a target.

Just when it seemed the bleakest, Mary looked up and saw a figure of a large man about 50 yards away. She screamed for him to help her. As he approached, he said nothing while Mary explained, "Can you please help me to my home? I can't walk and my husband can't help me. I only live a few houses down the block." Still saying nothing, he scooped up Mary and carried her in his arms to the house as Tony used his cane to follow them. Arriving at 1110 Wolf Street, Tony unlocked the door as the man carried Mary up the steps and into the spacious living room. He then gently placed her onto the sofa, about 20 feet from the door.

Mary and Tony were safely home.

Tony immediately turned to the man, at the sofa, and offered him money for his help. The stranger smiled and then spoke for the first time, saying, "Have a good night." Tony glanced at Mary, looked up again, and the man was gone! The glance at Mary took but a second, yet somehow the visitor traversed the living room and was nowhere to be seen.

They looked at each other in amazement.

The following day, their daughter, Terry Savarese, a retired nurse, arrived for her daily 9:00 a.m. visit. Not knowing what had transpired the night before, Terry took one look at her mom, found out what happened, and called 911. The ambulance took Mary to the hospital, where x-rays revealed that she had broken her pelvis in two places. She would spend the next two weeks in the hospital and one month in rehab before returning to her home.

Soon after she was admitted to the hospital, Mary made it a point to tell the family that she was saved by an "angel" whom she referred to as the "Good Samaritan Angel." The mysterious circumstances only made both her and Tony believe it even more. So did we all. Let's face it: If anybody deserved to be saved by an angel, it was Aunt Mary, whose devoutness was unquestioned.

Uncle Tony would pass away four years later, at the age of 92. Mary lived for nine more years after the incident and passed away at 97.

She was no doubt "picked up" again, this time at heaven's door, by Tony and his new buddy, Mary's Good Samaritan.

18

A Living Tribute

The "Mother" Plant

WHEN MY DAD, Henry, passed away on October 16th, 2004, at the age of 91, our loss was met with a wonderful outpouring of love and condolences. Family and friends showed their compassion in a number of wonderful ways. One example that I will always remember was receiving a sympathy "dish garden" from my employer. The garden consisted of a variety of houseplants, beautifully arranged in a large, glass bowl. Among the plants, a small African violet took its place amid God's lovely creations. As the days went by, it became clear to me that the little plant needed a change of scenery. It was too cramped surrounded by the others and, for it to flourish, it needed to "branch out" on its own, so to speak.

I had a history with African violets. My mother, Catherine, who passed away a few years before at 94, had the proverbial "green thumb." Her exploits in this area were legendary throughout the family. She once planted a lemon seed in a pot and ended up with the only three-foot lemon tree in southwest Philly. She would have herbs growing in her kitchen throughout the year. Her gardenias would fill the house with the most wonderful fragrance. However, her first love was her African violets. Mom had a way of "rooting" the stems and transplanting the rooted stem into the soil. From that procedure, a new plant would sprout. The process took months. I am proud to say that I learned her technique and used to love watching her take care of them and talk to them. Thankfully, it was always a one-way conversation!

So, after transplanting Dad's African violet plant into its own pot, I took care of it by giving it a western exposure in my office window, watering it every three or four days, and feeding it a Miracle-Gro solution every few weeks. Its progress was uncanny. In fact, it did so well that, in about a year, I decided to use it as a "host" plant and try Mom's rooting process. My plan was to help the plant reproduce in this manner and, should I be successful, give away any new plants to family and friends. I saw this as a way to honor both Mom and Dad; to keep their memories alive through the baby plants and the beautiful blue violets, some of God's loveliest blooms, that would certainly someday appear.

The rooting process was simple, but a bit painstaking. First, I had to ensure that the host plant was healthy enough to provide a good, strong stem to act as the "Mother" leaf. Secondly, the stem must then be placed in water for a period of four to six weeks before it would produce enough little roots from its bottom. At that time, the root system would be developed adequately enough for the stem to be transplanted into good soil in a clean pot. During the rooting process, the water level had to always be kept up. Then it took at least two months before the first baby leaf sprouted up through the soil, making the host leaf officially a mommy! Sometimes the baby leaf never developed, and I'd have to start the process all over again.

Happily, I was successful on my first attempt. I gave the new plant to my sister, Kathy, and it now rests prominently on the plant stand in her dining room. My second attempt failed. Many successes and a few failures followed over the next eight years, and I was happy to share the new plants with loved ones. Just after Christmas, 2011, I decided to try again. It was a joyful time for us, as our daughter-in-law was pregnant with our second grandson. The new baby was due to arrive in March to join his brother, who was then 2 ½. On March 7th, I transplanted the well-rooted stem into the new soil pot. Knowing it would take a minimum of two months for the first baby leaf to appear, I made sure to water it regularly and keep an eye on it as it sat upon my office windowsill.

About two weeks later, on March 20th, our new grandson joined the clan. He was welcomed with more than a few open arms as he made his arrival. Upon returning from the hospital, I went about my normal chores. I was going to have to water the stem in the pot, since I didn't do so the day before, after checking on the dampness of the soil. When I picked up the pot, I had to rub my eyes in disbelief, for looking right back at me was the transplanted leaf in addition to a brand-new baby leaf, just sprouted! I yelled out jubilantly. My wife, Luann, heard from upstairs, and she was ready to call 911 until I explained what had happened.

She didn't believe me.

That stem had only been in the soil for barely two weeks. It always takes *at least* two months for the baby leaf to sprout. The arrival of the baby leaf coincided with the arrival of our new baby boy, so the Lord provided two gifts on that day. Of course, that new plant went to our son and his wife, and our memories of Henry and Catherine live on by way of those beautiful African violets.

19

When an Impulse Pays Off

"Dave the Mailman's" Artistry

IN THE FALL of 2012, I saw a promo on PBS that looked pretty interesting. It was for an upcoming documentary, *Paesani: Italian Culture in Northeast Pennsylvania,* which would air on the following Saturday evening. Being the grandson of four Italian immigrants, I naturally had an interest in the subject, so I decided to give it a shot. The program was a joy!

It showed how a large group of Italians settled in the area around Scranton, Pennsylvania, mostly during the 1920s. It documented the hardships the people suffered while coming over in large, crowded, aged boats in the hope of finding a better life for their families.

The documentary included numerous interviews of people, most of them now elderly, who either emigrated themselves as children or had parents who did so. They related their personal stories of good and bad times in a way that made you feel you went through it with them. The program showed how the immigrants brought their culture regarding food, religion, and lifestyle, but always knowing that they were now proud Americans. One particular interviewee caught my eye and, in doing so, he gave me the opportunity to experience some of the most delightful times of my life.

Al Pisa was in his 80s when he appeared on the show from his home in the "Bunker Hill" section of Dunmore, Pennsylvania. As soon as I saw and heard him, I was reminded of my father's beloved cousin, Frank Fusco, who passed away years ago at his home in Warwick, Rhode Island. Like Frank, Al's personality filled the room. He shared his stories about his family experiences in a way that grabbed your attention and simply made you smile. When he spoke of his family, you could see the warmth and the light of his heart shine through. Al's wife, Angie, and son, Carlo, were also featured in the show. Carlo gave a succinct account of how his Bunker Hill neighbors all essentially came from the same mountain village in Italy, Guardia dei Lombardi. They were friends and family over there, and now they are friends and family over here.

The next day, my wife and I returned from breakfast after Sunday mass. Still thinking of how much I loved the *Paesani* documentary, on an impulse, I decided to tell Al Pisa how much I enjoyed him on the show. I reasoned, "How many 80-year-old Al Pisas can there be in Dunmore, Pennsylvania? I should be able to find Al by doing a people search on the computer." So, at 11:00 a.m., I Googled "Al Pisa, Dunmore, PA." The first listing showed Al Pisa, age 85! I called the number, and a lady answered.

"Hello, is this Angie?" I asked.
"Yes," she said, "who is this?"

I explained that I was just an Italian guy from Jersey who saw the show last night and wanted to tell Al how much I enjoyed him and his storytelling.

"Oh, ok. Hold on," Angie replied.

Al greeted me with a big "Hello," and we had a 30-minute conversation that covered everything from his resembling my cousin to why he called it "sauce" instead of "gravy." The conversation ended with me telling him that Robert DeNiro had better watch out because Al Pisa was on a roll and would probably become the next box-office attraction. He finished by making me promise that I'd come up to see him and, after doing so, we said goodbye. Five minutes later, my phone rang. The caller ID read, "Al Pisa," so I answered it and said, "What's up, Al?"

The caller replied, "No this isn't Al, it's his son, Carlo. I just wanted to thank you for calling. You made my father's day."

I told Carlo that I'd be in touch, and we would all arrange to have lunch in Scranton.

By then it was the next year. Al's family and mine had exchanged Christmas cards in December and, now being late May, it was a good time to make the arrangements to visit the Pisas. I called Carlo, said hello, and was greeted with a silent moment that was instantly troubling. Al had passed away just weeks before, and the family was grieving. After offering some words of comfort, I told Carlo that I still intended to honor my promise to Al, and we made a date to get together.

My friend, Bill Winarski, and I made the trip to Dunmore and had a wonderful lunch with Carlo and Angie at a local Italian (What else?) restaurant. He took us to see his buddies, who were volunteering their time doing maintenance at St. Rocco's church, and the whole visit was like spending time with your beloved family. Carlo told me about a tradition Al had each fall: He would host a bocce tournament for his friends at his house. This was a tradition that had gone on for years, and Carlo invited Bill and me to come back in the fall to attend. We did so and, boy, did we have a ball!

Adjacent to the bocce court was the gathering area. We enjoyed the food presented on a table under the large grapevine, including, but not limited to, salami, prosciutto, various cheeses, hot and sweet peppers, tomatoes, marinated eggplant, and crusty Italian bread. The layout rivaled the quality of hors-d'oeuvres you would hope for at a traditional Italian wedding. After hours of food, wine, laughs, hugs, and bocce (rules made up as you go), we sat down to a dinner fit for an Italian cruise ship. The meal was blessed by the local parish priest and ended with an incredible pastry display provided by Dave "the Mailman" Evanko. Dave makes his living as a mailman, but his passion is baking. Words can't describe his talent.

Bill and I, dubbed "The Jersey Boys," continue to make our annual October trip to attend what is now called the "Al Pisa Memorial Bocce Tournament." Carlo, his son Alfredo, Dave the Mailman, and about 25 other guys have become cherished friends through this event, and it feels as though I have known them all of my life.

Thank God for planting that impulsive thought in my mind, on that Sunday, to place that first call. The result has enriched my life. And God bless Al, who I know watches over his friends and family as he dwells in the house of Our Lord.

20

An Added Bonus

The Chapel Mates: Richie Millilo,
Joe Schofield, the Author and Patt Millilo

IN 1993, I made a commitment with the hope of gaining some spiritual benefits and ended up with much more. Our church, St. Charles Borromeo, had just completed construction of the "Perpetual Adoration Chapel." The chapel was built to provide a quiet place where parishioners and guests could go to pray and meditate in the presence of the consecrated Holy Eucharist, which we Catholics believe to be the actual body and blood of Jesus Christ. Since "perpetual" means without interruption, the church hoped that parishioners would volunteer to be "Chapel Guardians" and commit to praying in the chapel for one specific hour each and every week. For instance, every Monday, from 6:00 a.m. to 7:00 a.m. In this way, all of the one-hour time slots would be filled around the clock, seven days per week. When the call went out for volunteers, I thought it would be a good opportunity to get more in touch with my spirituality, so I offered to be one of the guardians. I was even happier about the decision when my 10-year-old son asked if he could join me ... quite a commitment for a kid that age.

We had an early Saturday morning prayer time and were joined by a few other parishioners who had made the same commitment: Joe Schofield, along with Richie Millilo and his wife, Patt. I didn't know them at first but, as time went on, we naturally spoke before and after our hour and became friendly. As the years passed, we found our friendships growing into meaningful relationships that would touch upon all aspects of our lives. We learned about each other's families. We celebrated the good news and comforted each other when misfortune occurred. We gave each other prayers, encouragement, and love during illnesses and rejoiced at the weddings of our children.

I had a special relationship with both Joe and Richie. My son and I would have breakfast with Joe every week after chapel time. Joe, who was about 15 years my senior, was like my big brother. He was a self-made success, rising from extremely humble beginnings to become a consummate businessman who earned the trust of his clients by thoughtfully guiding their financial decisions. Our breakfast topics ranged from family, sports, and world affairs to the economy and the pitfalls of investing in some financial instruments as opposed to others. I was thrilled to have my boy share this great time with such a good, learned man who was of the highest moral character. Unfortunately, in 2013, Joe became ill and couldn't attend chapel any longer. He eventually passed away in October of 2014.

Richie was a few years older than me, and Joe's absence from the chapel only caused us to become closer. He was a south Philly boy who was full of stories about the old neighborhood. He spent years running his family business and then held a very important position with a government contractor. This involved extensive traveling, as he regularly met with military officials at the highest level. Richie was also a courageous survivor with no fear of death. He endured a life-threatening illness for years but always bounced back. He gave thanks to God for his ability to do so and celebrated his good health. His attendance at the chapel was but one way he showed his appreciation.

Richie finally succumbed to his illness in June of 2014. I knew that his favorite adult beverage was a gin and tonic. When I visited him shortly before he died, I just happened to bring a bottle of gin, some tonic water, and enough cups (the nurses provided the ice) to accommodate Richie, his family, my wife, me, and our priest friend, Fr. Roberto "Tito" Ignacio. Richie, lucid and smiling, received the sacrament of the "Anointing of the Sick." After the anointing, with the doctor's ok, he sipped his favorite drink as we all joined in. The remaining gin and tonic were taken home by Richie's daughter, Donna, and shared by the family as a toast in his honor on the first anniversary of his death.

I continue to attend the chapel at the appointed time. My son, who was married in November of 2007, has moved out of the area and worships at his new church. There is at once emptiness and yet fullness in the chapel. In my mind's eye, I can still see Joe, eyes closed in deep meditation, and Richie, sitting next to Patt, reading from scripture or some other religious piece. The breakfasts that the three of us so anticipated are no more. Richie no longer shares his post-chapel cream doughnut and trips to the local yard sales with his beloved Patt. However, the fullness I feel is in the knowledge of the wonderful friendship that our wives now share. My wife, Luann, along with Patt, and Joe's wife, Rita, have taken up where the guys left off. And my heart is filled with the wonderful memories of two of my best buddies, who just happened to pick the same worship hour that I did. Rather than believe that was just a coincidence, I choose to believe that Divine Guidance put us there at the same time so that we could share each other's lives while getting a little closer to our Savior.

21

Hitting the Jackpot

Our Statue of St. Francis of Assisi

A FEISTY LITTLE creature lost its independence the day after the 4th of July, 2015, but ended up hitting the jackpot.

As I watched the ballgame on that lazy 4th of July afternoon, my concentration was shattered by my wife Luann's scream: "Charlie, there's a canary at our bird feeder!" She was looking out of the kitchen window and saw this little, yellow bird competing with sparrows, cardinals, and bluejays. Knowing the small bird had no chance to survive for long among those larger, more aggressive birds, I naturally had to go out there and try to save him. As I approached the feeding frenzy, I discovered that the "canary" wasn't a canary at all, but a six-month-old, green and yellow Australian budgie parakeet. Every time I got close to him, he took off. After four or five feeble attempts, I finally gave up, realizing he could fly a lot faster than I could run, and he wanted no part of me or captivity.

Upon waking the next morning, which was Sunday, I decided to say a little prayer to St. Francis of Assisi (we have a statue of him in our front garden), who is the patron saint of animals, and ask him to help me to figure out a way to catch this little guy. I clearly couldn't do it by myself, for it is a well-known fact that southwest Philly boys are not famous for their trapping skills.

Among our many bird feeders, we have several that are designed to allow small birds to go through an exterior, cage-like structure in order to reach the food. This unique design prevents larger birds and squirrels from eating everything before the little guys get their shot. Luann and I went out to breakfast early and, since we had attended mass on Saturday night, our Sunday obligation was fulfilled. Upon returning, she said she wanted to see the progress of my vegetable garden, in the rear of the house. While walking back there, I noticed that the parakeet was trapped inside one of the special bird feeders I just described. He had gotten in ok but couldn't figure out how to exit. It was now a simple task for us to catch him and make him the new member of our family. I was going to name him "Indy" since we first saw him on the 4th. However, I was overruled, as usual, in favor of the name "Sparky" (fireworks, sparklers, you know …).

St. Francis came through for us in a mighty way. Sparky would have certainly ended up a snack for a hawk or some other predator if he didn't starve to death first. Instead, this little guy lives the life of a king, with his own cage in a climate-controlled room, enjoying four different kinds of healthy food and the company of a very talkative, 20-year-old cockatiel named Nunzio.

Sounds like hitting the jackpot to me!

22

Nothing to Laugh About

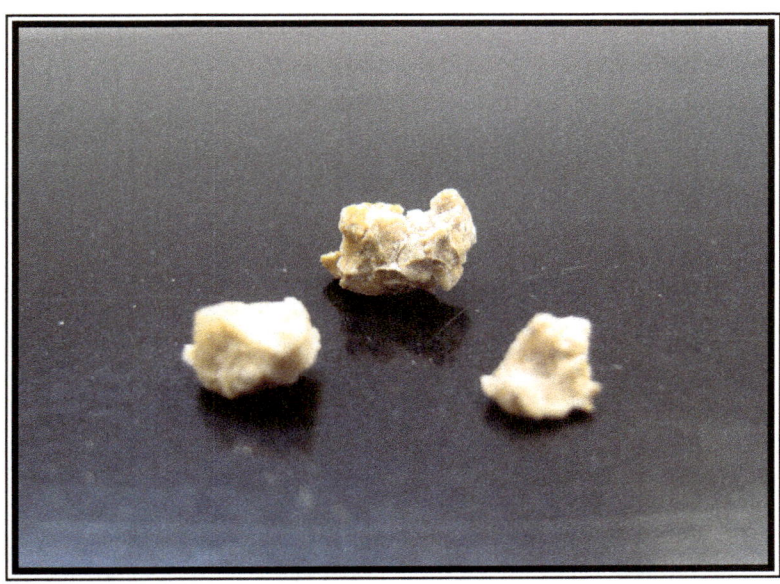

Actual Kidney Stones

I regard it as a strange phenomenon that begs questioning: *Why do people who shared a particular hardship or unpleasantness find humor in their suffering when discussed later?* Guys might stand around chuckling about a time their car broke down in the middle of nowhere or veterans may laugh about their experiences in Basic Training while in the care of a particularly brutal DI. I must admit that, on many occasions, I have laughed with others about a particular ailment I have endured twice that was anything but funny at the time. The events I speak of were two separate attacks of the dreaded kidney stones.

In the summer of 1984, I was living in Drexel Hill, Pennsylvania. As I dozed on my couch one peaceful Sunday night, I was awakened by a pain that radiated from my back into my groin. The sensation was horrifying. I had no idea what was causing it; I only knew I had never experienced that kind of pain before. I decided that I'd better get to the hospital. In an effort not to wake my wife or young kids, I struggled to my Chevy Malibu by myself and drove the half-mile to the Delaware County Hospital emergency room. Upon my arrival, the nurse took one look and made me put on a hospital gown. I waited for two auto-accident victims to be treated before the doctor got to me. By then, any modesty I may have had only an hour before was thrown out the window. I'm sure the nurses were treated to a few interesting sights as I thrashed around in the cubical, trying to alleviate the discomfort. Unfortunately, there is no position you can get into that will lessen the constant pain. Only a shot of morphine helped. I spent three days in the hospital before I "passed' the stones and was released. I was told that, if they do reoccur, it usually happens within 10 years or so.

Nine years later, I was living in New Jersey. It was ironic that I was about to make a sales call on my customer at the Hunterdon Medical Center in Clinton, New Jersey, about 60 miles from home. Deciding to get a quick bite first, I stopped into the local McDonald's and, while walking to my car, it happened again … that same terrible pain I had nine years earlier. This time, I knew what it was. I drove to the Center and staggered into my customer's office, explaining that I was having an attack. He said, "Let's go. I'll get you admitted." However, I turned him down, knowing that my wife would be worried, and the distance from home would only create problems. I decided to risk driving home and going to my local hospital in Cherry Hill. As I sped down Route 29, along the Delaware River, and later on Route 295, in an effort to make it back, I was hoping a state policeman would notice me and perhaps give me an escort. Of course, this made no sense at all but, at the time, logic was not at my fingertips as I drove with my teeth clenched while evoking the help of God the father, God the son, and the Holy Spirit, along with every Saint who came to mind. Miraculously, I made it back ok, squirming in my seat for the entire 60 miles. When I stumbled into the emergency room at Kennedy Memorial Hospital, I was so stressed that my blood pressure was through the roof, and it took three shots of morphine to calm things down.

For the first two days of my stay, the treatment involved, among other things, taking liquids orally and intravenously with the hope of my passing the stone or stones. When that didn't work, I was told that I had to have some x-rays taken with a full bladder. Now, the phrase "full bladder" sounds benign enough, don't you think? Well, when you have kidney stones, it is anything but. I can only describe it in this way:

1. Recall how much it hurt **the worst time** that you had to go to the bathroom but had to hold it in until you reached the facility.

2. Double it.

3. That's what it felt like with a **FULL** bladder.

I wasn't permitted to relieve myself - hence the bladder began to fill. Once the ultrasound showed that it was completely full, I was taken down to the lab to have the images taken. In I went, and a nice, young nurse explained to me that she would be taking pictures for about 45 minutes. I politely told her that she was crazy if she thought that I could last that long. The old bladder was starting to wave the white flag. After about 25 minutes of taking the x-rays, I couldn't stand it any longer. As I lay on the table, I told her:

"Honey, either you get me out of here, or there's going to be a big accident because I'm about to bust." She was kind enough to relent and handed me one of those little, portable urinals. It was as if she had given me a pot of gold. I was about to make quick use of it when three young nurses entered the room on their way to the lab office. I said, "Ladies, I'm sorry, but if you stay here, you are about to see a show you may not have bargained for." They just laughed and moved on. I put the urinal to good use, and I felt like the weight of the world was off my shoulders.

Two days later I was released, again apparently having passed the kidney stones. I say "apparently" because, in both in-stances, we never recovered the stones. They may have been so small that they slipped through the screening device used to capture them.

Now, over 20 years later, I haven't had an acute attack since.

But, invariably, when I come upon someone who has had kidney stones too, we exchange stories, and a few chuckles usually slip into the conversation. I guess those light-hearted moments are just one way to deal with a situation over which you had absolutely no control … And you'll never forget!

23

A Little "Miracle"

The Author's Beloved Rosary

IF ANY OF you think that God has no sense of humor, I invite you to talk to me. At least 60 years ago, probably around the time I made my Confirmation, I was given a set of basic black rosary beads. For those of you who are unfamiliar with them, I would simply describe rosary beads as a loop of interlocking beads which serve two purposes: They are used to represent the particular prayer you are saying, and they also allow you keep the count of the prayers. Each set has beads that represent the "Our Father," the "Hail Mary," and the "Glory be" prayers, and the beads are attached to one another by small, metal links. The "Hail Mary" beads are the most prevalent, numbering 50, composed of five strands of 10 beads each.

Those old rosaries have been everywhere with me. I've taken them on vacations, business trips, army bases, you name it. I am not a "white-knuckle" flyer, but I have always taken the prudent step to pray the rosary just prior to leaving the terminal and jumping on a jet. (Just in case.)

The age of the beads presents some problems. The attached crucifix has broken in half, although the small figure of Jesus remains completely intact. But the major issue is that the links tend to weaken and open, causing the beads to get tangled. Not being blessed with a great deal of patience, having to untangle the rosary beads tends to drive me a little crazy. I have let the knot of beads sit on my desk for weeks at a time after trying to untangle them for 10 or 15 minutes. Once a sufficient length of time has gone by, I give it another try and have always been successful.

However, about a year ago, something happened that I can't explain, and it had nothing to do with the normal tangling issue.

While at chapel one Saturday morning, I reached into my pocket to take out the rosary for prayer. As I pulled the beads out, I noticed that one link had opened up, so the beads were just dangling in a straight line, not in their normal circular configuration. To make matters worse, one of the "Hail Mary" beads had fallen off, leaving four groups of 10 beads and one group of nine. But the good news is that I recovered the detached bead, and the rest weren't tangled up at all, so I could simply re-attach the wayward bead, which would make the set whole again. I placed the rosary and single bead in my pocket and went home. Upon my arrival, I reached into my pocket to retrieve the set but, to my dismay, the disconnected bead was nowhere to found. It wasn't in my pocket, it wasn't on the floor, and it wasn't in my car. It was nowhere. I surmised that I must have dropped it in the chapel or it fell out of my pocket in the street. It sure wasn't in my house.

Biting the bullet, I made the decision to reattach the links and live with the rosary as-is. This would mean that I would have only nine beads on one of the groups, so I'd just say an extra "Hail Mary" to make up for the missing bead. I made the repair later in the week and put the rosary on my bureau. I also asked my wife to be alert, in case I somehow dropped the missing bead in the house.

Three days later, it was Saturday, and time for me to go to my usual hour of prayer at our chapel. I grabbed the beads, put them in my pocket, and off I went. As I sat in the chapel preparing to say the rosary, I reached into my pocket and removed them. Manipulating the beads to get a good grip, I couldn't help but be shocked when I saw that each of the five sections now had 10 beads! When I arrived home, I asked my wife if she had found the bead and reattached it. With a quizzical look on her face, she answered, "No." Then I told her what happened, and she was astounded. I, myself, have no answer. All that I know is that one bead was lost, and it was miraculously restored. Of that I am certain.

My only question is this: Did God laugh harder after He finished creating the camel or after He saw the look on my face when I discovered this little miracle?

24

Getting a Blessing the Hard Way

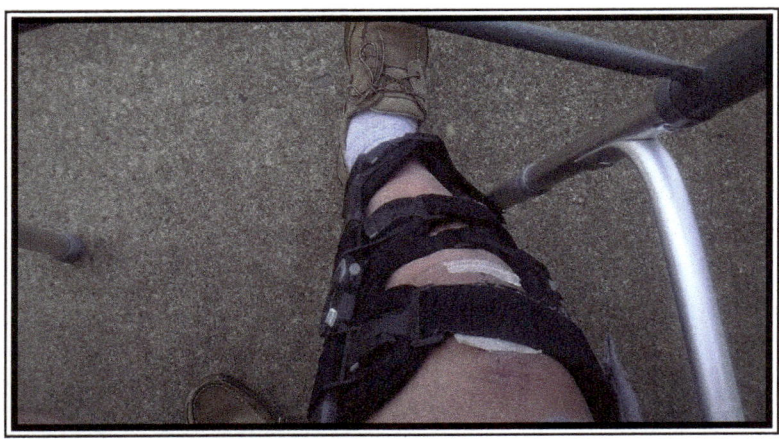

The Author's Repaired Knee, One Day Post-Op

MY DAUGHTER, ROSIE, and I have always enjoyed our annual baseball trips. She is a Phillies fan in the most sincere sense, and it's always fun when we go somewhere to watch them play. Included in those trips have been six jaunts to Clearwater, Florida, to see some Spring Training action. Originally, 2018 was to feature a return to Clearwater after a five-year hiatus in favor of seeing them play away games in Toronto, Cleveland,

Chicago, and Pittsburgh, and a great trip to the Baseball Hall of Fame in Cooperstown, New York. So the plans were all made to leave for Florida on March 21st for a relaxing, five-day trip to see four games in Clearwater, Lakeland, and Bradenton.

Yep, we were all set to go!

Sunday, the 18th, was three days prior to our departure. My wife and I attended mass, as usual, at 8:00 a.m. This also happened to be a day when our Holy Name Society sponsored one of their Pancake Breakfasts, held in the multi-purpose room inside the church. As we usually do, we decided to attend the breakfast so we could enjoy Aunt Jemima's creation and some pretty good sausages to keep the pancakes company. After the food and fellowship with the other parishioners, it was time to leave and get on with our day, which would later include a 6th birthday party for our grandson.

As we walked down the wide stairway leading to the main corridor of the church, I was about to step onto the last stair when I slipped and fell to the ground. As soon as I hit the floor, I knew I was in trouble, although, in that split second, my thoughts flew to how disappointed Rosie would be because there would be no trip to Clearwater this year. My leg was locked at the knee, and I couldn't straighten it out. Emergency services were called, and I was off to the hospital. Six hours later, I was sent home with a CT scan and x-rays which showed probable torn tendons and a small femur fracture at the top of the knee. I needed an MRI to get a better look in order to confirm the diagnosis. Two days later, the MRI revealed that I had ruptured three of my four quadriceps, and they would need to be surgically repaired.

As I awaited the scheduling of my surgery, I made all of the necessary calls to cancel the plane tickets, the hotel, and the car rental for the much-anticipated Phillies trip. I had purchased eight tickets, two for each of the games, and I wanted to make sure they were used. I emailed the four for the Clearwater games to a friend who lives there and who would have met us for dinner on the day we arrived in Florida. I decided to call the fire departments in Bradenton and Lakeland to see if any of their personnel would like to attend the games. It would be my honor to provide them.

I try to live a pretty faith-based life, so I don't make a habit of questioning why bad things sometimes happen to me. I'm really glad I didn't in this case because, out of this frustrating and very painful situation, I received a blessing in a matter of minutes from an unexpected source.

I Googled the Lakeland, Florida, fire department phone number and placed the call. A nice lady by the name of Ali Norton answered with a very friendly greeting. She listened as I explained the situation and my intentions regarding the tickets. She was very appreciative and said she was sure that someone there would want to use them. I suggested that she do so since the game was to be played on Saturday, the 24th. Ali shared with me that she would love the tickets but would like to give them to her son, whose birthday was on the 26th. I said, "Sure, Ali, go ahead and do that." She thanked me several times, saying she wished she could repay the kindness. I replied, "You can repay me by saying a prayer for me that my surgery goes well." She assured me she would, and we said goodbye after I asked her to let me know when the email with the tickets arrived ok.

In an email, Ali confirmed that she was able to print the tickets. And then she wrote:

"Mr. Sacchetti,

"I pray that everything goes well with your surgery. Here's your prayer:

"LORD,

"We ask You to give Mr. Sacchetti peace with this surgery that he will go through. Thank You that You blessed him with the great skills and wisdom of his doctor. We pray that this surgery will be a success, and please bless him in each step of his recovery process. Protect the wounds from infection, heal and restore any damaged areas, and help him rest, knowing that You are there with him to help him recuperate.

"In Your name we pray, Jesus,

"Amen.

"Take care, Mr. Sacchetti, and be careful!

"Ali"

It's hard for me to explain how touched I was after I read that prayer from a total stranger who took the time to express her petitions in such a loving and sincere way. In the weeks that followed, I was blessed with many such prayers from friends and family alike.

After the successful surgery on March 26th, my leg had to be immobilized for two weeks while the healing began. I would also wear a brace for nine weeks, day and night, to ensure I did not hyperextend my still-unstable knee area. Finally, I started a physical therapy program that lasted eight weeks.

As the therapy continued, my therapist was amazed at the speed of my recovery. After two weeks, I was able to shed my walker and cane. I could drive after three weeks. After six weeks, my surgeon expressed similar amazement. Two and a half months after surgery, I am now walking normally but prudently look for handrails when I negotiate steps! As a 71-year-old, I certainly have no extraordinary physical strength. What I *did* have was the powerful prayers of many loving people who asked God to guide my every step during surgery and recovery. For that, I am grateful.

25

Love's Legacy

Henry and Catherine Sacchetti

I'M ONE OF those guys who believes in an afterlife. Being raised as and still a practicing Catholic, after 71 years, I look forward to eternity in heaven. One of my main hopes is that, when I finally get there, I shall be greeted with a big,

"Welcome home, Charlie," by the multitude of family and friends that have preceded me. It's really a pretty simple concept for me. I was put on this earth to love my God, to live my life as best I could, to be a good husband, to raise good children, and to help others along the way. I figure if I do all of those things, Jesus, my Lord and Savior, will be happy to see me. The fact that He died to save me makes my ending up in heaven a no-brainer. As I grow older, I also think more and more about the meaning of the word "legacy," which is the "handing down" of something. As I've thought about it, I've come to understand that one's legacy may include more than you ever realize.

I started thinking about my deceased parents, Henry and Catherine, in this regard on January 23rd, 2018, the day that marked their 81st wedding anniversary. I wonder if they, in their spiritual existence, can fully realize what they left as their legacy of love. When Mom passed away in 2002, they had been married for 65 years. Their progeny includes two married children, four grandchildren, and four great-grandchildren. Each of my parents knew their responsibility to the marriage and to the family. In those days, roles were clearly defined. Dad worked and earned money to support the family, and Mom did mostly everything else regarding the home. She cooked, cleaned, shopped, paid the bills, and, most importantly, raised the kids. When we were growing up, it was unusual for the wife to work outside of the home. Luckily for the many kids we knew, our middle-class neighborhood was chock full of "housewives" who were more than happy to accept the role my mother filled so well.

Neither of our parents ever attended college, but they were

both natural teachers. My sister and I learned, at an early age, the absolute obligation to attend church on a weekly basis. As the son, I was the recipient of many other lessons from my father. He taught me about work ethic, accepting responsibility, dealing with adversity, and the importance of fairness, respectfulness, and honor. My sister, Kathy, learned a lot from Mom. Fortunately for her family, she inherited Mom's talent for cooking. She also learned how to be a selfless mother and a fierce guardian of her children. We learned firsthand the benefits of discipline and how well it worked when used at the right time. There were no "timeouts" when we were kids. The only discipline-related elapsed time I ever knew fell between the grabbing of the belt and its contact with my lower extremity. While today the very thought of administering corporal punishment is considered a near-capital crime by some "enlightened" ones, I am proud to repeat a line I have often used to describe my loving, Sicilian mother:

"Mom was only five feet tall and never played baseball in her life, but she could hit you with a shoe from 20 feet away."

It's important to note that I cannot recall one time when I didn't deserve the discipline I received.

I hope, as Mom and Dad gaze down upon those who share their DNA, they feel God's peace and a sense of accomplishment. They left behind a loving group of people, all with varying compositions of their inherited traits and talents. My parents' spirits live within us. and I'm happy to say that we speak of them frequently, ensuring that they are not just abstract characters to our grandchildren, who never had the opportunity to meet them in the flesh.

CPSIA information can be obtained
at www.ICGtesting.com
Printed in the USA
BVHW090221120119
537672BV00007B/95/P